Making
Ceramic Sculpture

Making Ceramic Sculpture

Techniques
■
Projects
■
Inspirations

Raúl Acero

LARK BOOKS

A Division of Sterling Publishing Co., Inc.
New York

Editor: **Deborah Morgenthal**
Art Director: **Kathleen Holmes**
Assistant Editor: **Heather Smith**
Production Assistance: **Thom Gaines, Hannes Charen**
Photography: **Evan Bracken**

Library of Congress Cataloging-in-Publication Data

Acero, Raúl.
    Making ceramic sculpture : techniques, projects, inspirations / Raúl Acero.
        p.   cm.
    Includes bibliographical references and index.
    ISBN 1-57990-175-1
    1. Ceramic sculpture—Technique.   2. Ceramic sculpture—Pictorial works.   I. Title.
NK4235.A26 2000
731.4—dc21   00-030169

10 9 8 7 6 5 4 3 2 1

Published by Lark Books, a division of Sterling Publishing Co., Inc.
387 Park Avenue South, New York, N.Y. 10016

© 2001, Raúl Acero

Distributed in Canada by Sterling Publishing, c/o Canadian Manda Group, One Atlantic
Ave., Suite 105, Toronto, Ontario, Canada M6K 3E7

Distributed in the U.K. by Guild of Master Craftsman Publications Ltd.
Castle Place 166 High Street, Lewes, East Sussex, England, BN7 1XU
Tel: (+ 44) 1273 477374 Fax: (+ 44) 1273 478606
Email: pubs@thegmcgroup.com
Web: www.gmcpublications.com

Distributed in Australia by Capricorn Link (Australia) Pty Ltd., P.O.   Box 6651, Baulkham
Hills, Business Centre, NSW 2153, Australia

If you have questions or comments about this book, please contact:
Lark Books
50 College St.
Asheville, NC 28801
(828) 253-0467

Manufactured in Hong Kong

ISBN 1-57990-175-1

From left to right: **Leahy Hardy**, (p. 115),
Michael Messina (p. 108), **Elyse
Saperstein** (p. 95), **Aurore Chabot** (p.
125), **Ann Marie Perry** (p. 113)

Upper right: **Laura Wilensky**, (p. 111)

CONTENTS

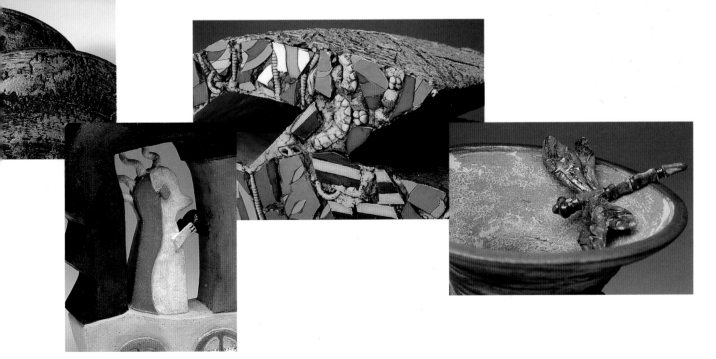

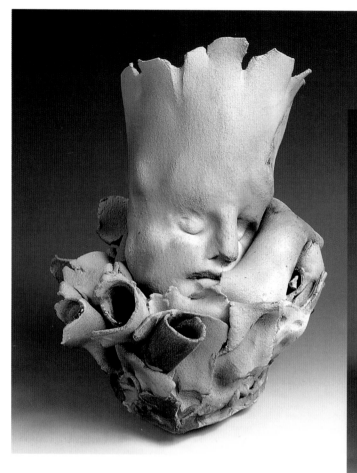

Top left and right: **Raúl Acero**, *Heart's Needle*, 1997.
14 x 20 x 12 inches (36 x 51 x 31 cm). Raku; slab
built; glazes, raku fired. Photo by Evan Bracken

Bottom left and right: **Raúl Acero**, *Ruinas*, 1992.
22 x 20 inches (56 x 51 cm). White earthenware; slab
built; ceramic stains; oxidation fired, Δ3. Photo by artist

INTRODUCTION

Ceramic sculpture is an ancient and beloved art form. Clay has been used by people for hundreds of years not only to make vessels but also to create sculptures. Some of the best records we have of ancient peoples are preserved for us in their clay work. I think all human beings are born with the ability and the desire to make art. Slowly, over time, and due to our education, we lose those abilities and replace them with insecurities about making and understanding art. I would like to take you back a little bit and show you how you might recapture your birthright—your natural ability to sculpt forms in clay.

In this book are a few projects and some instructions on how to go about forming these sculptures.

They require little in the way of tools, because the most important tools are the ones you bring to the work: namely, your desire to create, your time, and your natural talent. Every one of us sees things differently—I mean this literally; one person will see shapes and colors differently from another person. We are all different, and this means we will all make different artwork.

Raúl Acero, *Small Paradise*, 1993. Four pieces, each 14 x 28 inches (36 x 71 cm). Raku; glazes, wood, mixed media; raku fired. Photo by Evan Bracken

7

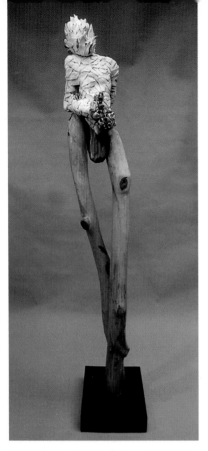

After looking at the projects and before trying them, remember this: your piece will be different...it will be yours!

The greatest value lies in the doing—in the making of the work—and less in the final product. It's the time spent enjoying the clay and the moment of sculpting that enriches you. As you spend more time working with clay, you will become more proficient with the techniques, you will understand the clay better, and you will enjoy the moments even more. It will come as no shock to you that the world is a fast-paced, strange, and often stressful place. I invite you to step into another world, an older and slower one, where what counts is precisely that...going slowly, calming down, leaving judgements behind, and creating things in clay...for yourself.

Raúl Acero, *Votive Figure*, 1992. 72 x 14 x 10 inches (1.8 m x 36 cm x 25 cm). Stoneware; slab and pinch built; terra sigillata with glazes; oxidation fired, Δ2. Photo by artist

Left: **Raúl Acero**, *Pescadito (Little Fish)*, 1993. 26 x 18 inches (66 x 46 cm). Raku; slab built; raku fired with terra sigillata. Photo by artist

Above: **Raúl Acero**, *Ceramic Head*, 1986. 24 x 16 x 18 inches (61 x 41 x 46 cm). Stoneware; pinched clay over armature; red iron wash; oxidation fired to Δ4. Photo by artist

GETTING STARTED

Jenny Mendes, *The Bird Balancer*, 1999. 19 x 9 x 9 in. (48.3 x 22.8 x 22.8 cm). Terra cotta with grog; coil built from slab; carved and painted with terra sigillatas, black commercial underglaze; fired in electric kiln, Δ1. Photo by Heather Protz

Laura Wilensky, *Smile (taxus teapot, nonfunctional)*, 1998. 7¼ x 10¼ x 7 in. (18.3 x 25.5 x 17.5 cm). Porcelain; handbuilt; handpainted underglazes, underglaze stains, china paints; fired in electric kiln, Δ10, Δ018. Photo by Storm Photo

THERE IS A GREAT DEAL to learn about clay: the different types and properties of clay; why there are so many firing temperatures; what type of kiln best suits the glazes you are using—to name a few. If you're a beginning ceramicist, you may be confused by all this information. That's why I want to start out as simply as possible. After all, the important thing is to be able to make sculptures, not to become on expert on the minerals found in different types of clay.

My goal in this section of the book is to provide you with basic information that will enable you to make ceramic sculpture in your home, pretty much right away. I can recommend a few books I like that thoroughly cover the technical aspects of ceramics (see page 143); I urge you to look at several. The glossary (page 137) also offers more detailed information.

HOME STUDIO

It's easy to set up a work area in which you can create ceramic sculpture. I have made sculpture in all kinds of unlikely spaces and places, from a table in a city apartment to a field of grass in the country. Garages, basements, and attics are perfectly useable, as are porches and covered patios. One important criterion is that the work space be well-ventilated. You'll want to minimize exposure to clay dust and glaze chemicals, so it's important to keep your work space as far as possible from the kitchen and other living areas. It helps to have a water source nearby, or you'll soon tire of carrying buckets of water to your work area.

Important ecological advice: Never pour water containing clay and glazes directly into your drainage system, whether it's a public system or a septic tank.

When you recycle dry clay, use the water left over from rinsing your hands and tools; let the rest of the clay water evaporate, and dispose of the sediment in the trash. Dispose of leftover water from rinsing glazing tools in the same manner.

Install as much open shelving as you can afford: to a ceramicist, there's no such thing as too many shelves. You will need a sturdy work table that allows you to reach your sculpture from all four sides and doesn't wiggle when you pound on it. Keep your work area clean and clear of clay dust by cleaning with a damp sponge and mopping frequently. Did I mention how important proper ventilation is? Try not to kick up a lot of clay dust by

Above: **Kathi Roussel**, *Lifeform*, 1998. 42 x 9 x 9 in. (106.8 x 22.8 x 22.8 cm). Low-fire white clay; wheel-thrown, handbuilt; fired in electric kiln, Δ6.

Right: **Pamela Timmons**, *Turtle*, 1999. 7 x 11 x 13 in. (17.8 x 28 x 33 cm). Stoneware; head sculpted, hollowed; shell hump molded, altered; body slab and coil constructed; oxidation fired, Δ6. Photo by Jim Wolnosky

sweeping or brushing. There's more about safety on page 135, and I urge you to read it.

Don't let anyone discourage you by saying you need a huge work space or a lot of specialized tools in order to make ceramic sculpture. You really don't. What you do need to get started is the willingness to invest time in yourself and the desire to explore your own creativity. More important than any tool is your passion to discover what you can sculpt with clay, and a commitment to nurture yourself through this exploration.

BODY LANGUAGE

When you make ceramic sculpture, your hands will become one of your most important tools. Working with clay dries out your skin, so keep a large bottle of lanolin or other moisturizer on hand. Your whole body is really a tool, too, so it's a good idea to get in or stay in good physical condition.

HAND TOOLS AND SUPPLIES

For the ceramic sculptor, wooden modeling tools are invaluable: you really can't do a good job without them. They can be purchased at any good art-supply store or by mail order from ceramic-supply houses. Buy a variety of shapes; they don't cost very much. You'll soon discover your favorites, which you'll soon misplace, if you're like me; so buy two of your favorites.

The other tools and supplies you'll need for ceramic sculpture are simple and include household items, such as plastic bowls, cardboard tubes, and newspapers. Here's a list of some items that are good to have on hand:

~ **Cutting wire.** Length of wire with small dowel handles, used for slicing slabs from a block of soft clay or for cutting leather-hard clay.

Leah Hardy, *Fruition*, 1999. 11.5 x 8.5 x 3 in. (28.8 x 21.3 x 7.5 cm). Earthenware; slab-built, hand-modelled; ceramic doors attached with brass hinges (post-firing); low-fire glaze, terra sigillata and oxides fired in electric kiln, Δ04.
Photo by artist

~ **Fettling knife.** Tapered knife used for cutting soft and leather-hard clay.

~ **Pin tool.** Needle with a handle for cutting thin slabs and for trimming and piercing air bubbles in soft clay.

~ **Rib.** Wood, metal, or plastic rib, with straight edge and curve for shaping soft clay.

~ **Serrated rib.** Flexible metal rib for scraping, scoring, and texturing soft, leather-hard, and dry clay.

~ **Fork.** Kitchen fork for scoring and texturing soft and leather-hard clay.

~ **Wooden modeling tools in various sizes and shapes.** For modeling and sculpting soft and leather-hard clay.

~ **Wooden paddle.** For shaping clay.

~ **Wooden rolling pin or fat wooden dowel.** For rolling out slabs of clay.

~ **Ribbon tool.** Tool with square and looped metal ribbon ends for trimming and hollowing soft and leather-hard clay.

~ **Wire loop tool.** Tool with looped metal wire ends for hollowing and sculpting soft clay.

~ **Sponges.** Synthetic sponge for cleanup. Natural sponge for smoothing out rough surfaces on soft, leather-hard, or dry clay.

~ **Turntable.** Allows you to work on piece from all sides.

~ **Small pieces of wood.** For placing work on to lift it from the work surface.

~ **Spray bottle.** For keeping clay moist.

~ **Plastic bags.** For clay storage.

~ **Plumber's propane torch.** For speeding up the clay-drying process.

~ **Rubber gloves.** To wear when working with glazes.

~ **Assorted paintbrushes.** For applying stains and glazes.

~ **Scale.** For measuring water and glazes.

Bacia Edelman,
Blue-Striped
Skipper, 1999. 9½
x 19 x 4 in. (24.3 x
48.3 x 10 cm).
Mid-range
stoneware; pierced,
handbuilt; slips,
sprayed crawl
glazes; multi-fired
in electric kiln,
Δ04, Δ06.
Photo by artist

The photo below shows some of these basic tools and supplies. You can purchase the more specialized items, such as the potter's fettling knife and the pin tool, at art- or ceramics-supply stores. For other tools, you can improvise. For example, I have used wooden spoons purchased at a grocery store as paddles; gourmet stores have even more interesting spoons and wooden cooking utensils. If you have a friend who likes woodworking, he could make you paddles from scrap wood.

Clockwise: Paintbrush, wooden paint stirrer, ribbon tool, wooden modeling tools, fettling knife, and assorted rib tools

KILNS

There is one tool that is indispensable; without it you cannot make ceramic art. That is, the kiln. A kiln is really just an oven, but a special one. It goes to very high temperatures and is designed to keep as much heat as possible inside. A distinguishing factor with regard to kilns is what kind of fuel they use. This breaks down into two categories, fossil fuels or electricity.

FOSSIL FUEL KILNS

Fossil fuel kilns are ones that use gas, wood, or some other carbon-based fuel to fire with. Electric kilns create heat by resistance, and so nothing is burned—they are like giant toasters. Gas-fired kilns have the advantage of creating an atmosphere brought on by the burning of the fuel. This atmosphere is one of reduced oxygen, hence the phrase "reduction firing," as when a potter saunters up to you and asks "Was that piece reduced?" He is not asking if the piece got smaller; he wants to know if it was fired in a reduced oxygen atmosphere. Electric kilns, on the other hand, don't burn anything; so they fire in an oxygen-rich atmosphere called "oxidation firing." That same potter who asks if your piece was "oxidized," is not offering to perform CPR: he is asking if it was fired in an oxidation atmosphere.

ELECTRIC KILNS

In urban areas it's more common to find electric kilns than gas-fired ones. You can find gas kilns in colleges and universities in the city and wood-fired kilns out in the country. An electric kiln then has distinct advantages: all you need is a special 220-volt electric line and somewhere to put the kiln. Did I mention price? Large electric kilns can be very expensive; smaller ones cost much less; and used kilns often can be purchased at reasonable prices. To give you an idea of available sizes: A large electric kiln measures 35 x 42 inches (90 x 107 cm) while a small one measures 25 x 28 inches (64 x 71 cm). Electric kilns work well in a garage or basement and are relatively easy to fire. Some are even computer-assisted to help you fire.

Lacking the money to invest in a kiln, you will likely seek out an institution or individual who has one. Most ceramic studios will fire your work for a small fee. Sometimes it's a good idea to take a class at a school or ceramic studio and get to know the system and the clay they use. No matter how or where you wind up firing your piece, knowing the type of clay you're using and its temperature is a necessary pre-requisite to successfully getting the ceramic piece fired. For a complete discussion of the different types of clay and clay-firing temperatures, see page 22.

CHAPTER TWO

CLAY BASICS

Pat Cronin, *Reliquary*, 1999. 9 x 1 x 4 in. (22.9 x 2.5 x 10.2 cm). Raku clay; handbuilt, textured; bisque fired, Δ04; reliquary glazed and wiped for line deposits with copper matt, base unglazed, blackened by carbon in reduction. Photo by John Bonath (Mad Dog Studio)

IT'S IMPORTANT TO SAY a few things about the techniques described in this book for creating forms with clay. The thing that distinguishes ceramic sculpture from other forms of sculpture (in addition to the fact that it's made of clay) is that generally it is built hollow. It follows then that all of the techniques used to work the clay focus on how to build a hollow form. Each technique does a different thing, and each can be mixed with another to get to the important part—making ceramic sculpture. Let's briefly review the techniques used to shape clay.

attaching them to each other. Coils are also used to create shapes and decoration to be applied to a form. The Bird on a Tree Pedestal on page 46 shows how to do this.

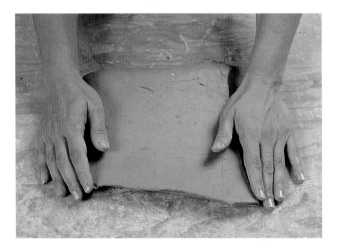

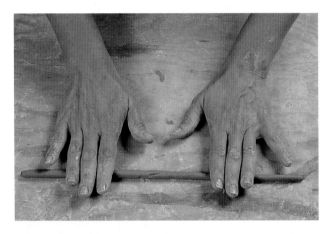

SLAB

This is one of my favorite techniques and a very useful one. It involves rolling out a sheet of clay, called a *slab*, and then constructing forms with it. Some people use a large machine called a *slab roller* to do this, but I know a few easier ways to do it without large machines. The photos above demonstrate the technique of *throwing out* a slab on a work surface to prepare it. The Head in Clay on page 70 and Standing Figure on page 80 demonstrate how to work with slabs.

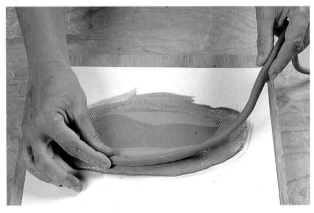

COIL

Coiled work involves rolling out clay in a ropelike shape called a *coil*. The technique is straightforward and useful for building up a thin-walled sculpture. You simply roll out a coil and attach it to a base. You roll out another coil and attach it to the first one, building the sculpture coil upon coil, creating the shape as you go. Then you wait a little while for the coils to stiffen a bit before

Louise Radochonski, *How Diaphanous It Is*, 1998. 12 x 7 x 8 in. and 10 x 6 x 12 in. (30 x 17.5 x 20 cm and 25 x 15 x 30 cm). Porcelain; solid, carved elements glued to hollow (pinch pots), carved elements; salt fired, Δ10. Photo by Tom Mills

PINCH

Pinching is one of the most basic of all clay techniques and a valuable one to learn. It involves putting your thumb into a round ball of clay and then pinching against the walls of the clay as you rotate it in your other hand. As with most things in visual art the written description seems more difficult than the actual technique. Look at the bird project (page 46) to see how this is done.

ATTACHING CLAY PIECES

When you attach soft clay pieces to one another to build ceramic sculpture, generally you use a serrated rib tool to score the end of the clay piece, brush on a coat of slip to the scored area, and attach the piece to what you're making. Throughout the projects, you'll be instructed to score and slip, score and slip. That's all there is to it. But sometimes it's not so easy nor convenient to score the pieces. In these instances, I use a mixture of Epsom salts and slip that acts as a flocculent and helps hold the clay together. I often eliminate scoring in the sculptures

and just use this attaching slip mixture instead. This method helps me be spontaneous in the making of a piece.

All you need to do is mix 1 heaping tablespoon of Epsom salts with about 1 cup of clay slip made from the same clay body as your sculpture. Add a few tablespoons of hot water and mix well. This will produce a nice thick, creamy attaching slip. Use a paintbrush to apply a generous amount of the mixture.

WARM-UPS

It's a good idea to get used to the clay before starting one of these projects, especially if you have no experience working clay. First, get your work space ready, find a comfortable chair, and get a good light source—a lamp, work light, or even better, natural light. Open the bag of clay and take a peek inside. Generally, commercial clay comes in a rectangular form—that's how it comes out of the mixer, and that's your first clue as to the nature of clay. It takes the form of whatever it's packed into. Now peel down the sides of the bag, reach in, and pinch off a piece of clay about the size of a lemon. Look closely at it, and, those among you who are brave, take a little whiff.

How does it smell? Does it feel cool? Press your thumb into the clay and then remove it. Notice your thumb print in the clay. That's how wonderful a material clay is; it's so receptive to touch that it records all kinds of texture.

Now close your eyes, roll the clay in your hands, and squeeze it gently. Take a deep breath; relax. Just sit still for a moment and breathe slowly and deeply. Open your eyes! Roll the clay between your hands and shape it into a ball. Hold it in the palm of your left hand (of your right hand, if you are left-handed) and take your right thumb and push it into the center of the clay ball—don't pierce it all the way through. Now gently turn the clay clockwise in the palm of your hand as you gently squeeze the wall between your right thumb and the middle finger of your right hand. Keep doing this until the wall gets thin. Remember to slow down and relax as you do this. Try to spend at least five minutes to complete the exercise. You might realize just how long a time five minutes is when you devote yourself to this exercise. If you rush, though, you also might realize just how much we rush through everything. This little exercise, this little clay object, can help you slow down…and relax.

Make a few of these pieces, let them stiffen a little, and then try assembling them into larger forms. Try to warm up like this each time you begin work. In this way you can remember to slow down and not make your clay work one more personal challenge, one more job to be dispatched. It's a good thing to take a few moments to establish contact with your senses and your spirit through the clay.

While we're on the subject of spirit, inspiration or the lack of it seems to be a topic often discussed in relation to art. There are even quite a few books devoted to discovering the artist within you. I think this book will give you the opportunity to make sculpture in a step-by-step manner. In so doing, you'll learn to handle clay and gain confidence. In due time, you'll probably begin to think about making your own, original sculptures.

Inspiration for these objects comes from within and without. Direct observation of the world around you in a new and distinct way is possible once you begin to see the shapes that make up the world as sculptural shapes. By combining different shapes, you can make nonfigurative or abstract pieces. Many times the expression of strong emo-

tions can best be captured by nonfigurative means—for example, by using strong shapes or by contrasting a small shape with a powerful or even threatening one. If figurative work interests you, then begin to observe the people around you. Try to focus on how different shapes make up the human body or head. Try sketching people while you're sitting at an outdoor cafe or on a bus or train. Of course, be prepared for conversation should you do this—people are interested in what artists do.

Internal inspiration can come at any time. Often, after you have some experience with making sculpture, you'll dream up shapes or artworks. Sometimes these images come to us before sleep, during dreams, or just before waking. These images can become an integral part of the art we make and are a welcome by-product of the kind of awakening that can come when you discover your potential as a human being and an artist. These inner visions that help us create art don't have to be grandiose—they can be small and humble—but they can be yours, and that is the grandest thing of all.

THE STAGES OF CLAY

The truth is, not all clays are the same. The type of clay you use (and the stage at which you work with it) will affect the look of the finished sculpture. Clay has several stages of dryness, and at each stage, the clay has certain traits. This subject could fill an entire book. But since we're here to get our hands on clay and to discover how easy it is to create sculpture, here's an overview of the basic stages of clay—definitely enough to get you started. Remember, artists of long ago created successful ceramic sculptures without reading a single book on the topic! Now it's your turn to sculpt.

DAMP

At this stage, the clay is malleable and plastic. It can be shaped, bent twisted, and sculpted. This is a good time for active surface effects, such as running your fingers across the surface to make impressions, or pressing fabric, paper, or stamps onto the surface. You can maintain clay at this stage almost indefinitely by keeping it covered tightly with plastic. Don't use dry-cleaning plastic—I have found that it lets air in! If you want to keep the clay really damp, cover it with a damp, not wet, paper towel, in a plastic bag. The paper towel will release moisture into the bag. You don't need to drape a heavy wet towel over your sculpture; this will only weaken the clay or remove surface detail.

LEATHER HARD

In this stage, the clay has lost water and is stiffer and harder. You can still see the fresh-looking color of the clay. It feels cold to the touch. The clay is too dry to bend without cracking but is still moist enough that you can incise the surface to create texture. This is a good time to add on pieces, cut and carve, paint on colored slips (engobes), or apply terra sigillata (see Surface Decoration, page 27). This is also a good time to transport the piece: it's stronger now than it will be when it's completely dry.

BONE DRY (GREEN)

Now the clay has lost all its "visible" water. It looks dusty, a little drab, and is usually lighter in color. The clay feels cool or warm to the touch. You cannot add clay to it at this time. Fresh, damp clay will not stick to dry clay; as soon as the damp clay loses water, it shrinks away from the dry piece and cracks. Some potters refer to *greenware* as any unfired clay object, whether leather hard or bone dry.

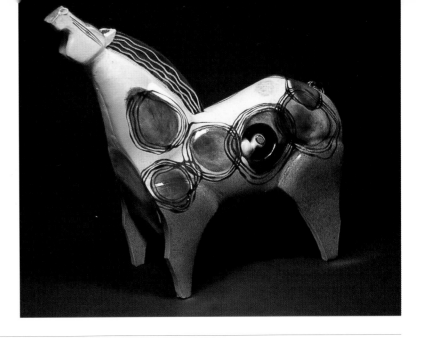

Far Left: **Joe Szutz**, *Untitled*, 1999. 14 x 15 x 5 in. (35 x 38 x 12.5 cm). Earthenware and terra-cotta mix (high grog content); coil and slab built; slips, stains; bisque fired in electric kiln, Δ04; multiple firings, Δ04. Photo by Bart Kasten

Left: **Jenny Mendes**, *Two Faced Rae*, 1998. 12 x 8 x 5 in. (30.5 x 20.3 x 12.8 cm). Terra cotta with grog; coil built from slab, pinched; terra sigillata, white and black underglaze; carved sgraffito lines; bisque fired , Δ06; glaze fired in electric kiln, Δ1. Photo by Heather Protz

Right: **Julie B. Hawthorne**, *Waterspot*, 1999. 24 x 25 x 12 in. (60 x 62.5 x 30 cm). Commercial white clay; wheel-thrown, hand-drolled, handbuilt; slips, engobes; clear glaze fired, Δ6. Photo by Chris Hawthorne

THE IMPORTANCE OF SLOW DRYING

These stages are all dictated by water content. Right out of the bag, 50 to 60 percent of the content of the clay is water. As the water evaporates out of the clay, the clay becomes progressively stiffer and smaller (yes, friends, it shrinks!) until it dries out completely. As it stiffens, it loses plasticity and strength until it finally becomes fragile, dried mud. The clay will not regain strength until it's fired. If all the water is not dried out of the clay before it's fired, that remaining water will turn to steam and rapidly seek an exit. The result is that your work will blow up—not the artistic impact you are striving for.

Water is also an intrinsic part of the clay on a molecular level; the chemical formula for clay includes H_2O. This means there is "invisible" water lurking in the clay itself, apart from the "visible" water used to mix up the clay. This invisible water needs to be driven out of the clay slowly during the firing, especially in the early stages of the firing. Actually, there are two ways to blow up your work: one involves firing a piece that is wet or damp; the other involves firing a piece that is dry but firing it too quickly.

How can you be sure the clay is dry? Here's another hard truth: you can't be 100 percent sure. By this I mean that I am unaware of any scientific test. But there are some common sense things you can do to encourage the piece to dry slowly and to determine how dry it is. First of all, make sure the sculpture dries for a while without being covered with plastic. Place slats of wood under the piece to allow air to circulate around it. Then look closely at the clay to see if has lost its "visible" water; make sure it looks dusty, dry, and light in color. Finally place the back of your hand, the inside of your wrist, or better yet (if you can) your cheek against the clay. If it feels pretty cold, that's a good indication that it's not yet completely dry and still contains water. As clay dries and gives off water, it produces a cool surface.

Always place your work on small pieces of wood, such as pine or plywood. This way, you can move it from place to place with out touching the piece itself. Always place newspaper under the sculpture so it doesn't stick to the wood. Try to do the final drying in a warm and dry area: leaving it uncovered in a warm, toasty room will most assuredly dry it out.

If you're having a piece fired at a school studio or ceramic shop, you are at the mercy of the person firing the kiln, and you run the risk of your piece being fired too quickly. To minimize that risk, make sure your piece is dry before giving it up for firing. If your piece is small and relatively thin walled, you should have no problems. Larger and

Marilyn Andrews, *Shutters*, 1998. 12 x 9 x 8 in. (30 x 22.5 x 20 cm). Stoneware; handbuilt; fired in electric kiln, Δ5. Photo by Bob Barrett

Beverly Crist, *Late Bloomer*, 1996. 19 x 12½ x 9 in. (47.5 x 31.3 x 22.5 cm). Terra cotta; handbuilt body; twigs pulled; bisque and glaze fired in electric kiln, Δ04. Photo by Mike Pecorino

more complex pieces are more likely to blow up if they are fired too quickly.

Most of the time I like to fire my sculpture by itself, without other pottery in the kiln. I place my piece inside the kiln, and with the top propped open and the kiln on the lowest setting possible, preheat the kiln overnight. Then the next day I do the actual firing. I find that this approach really drives off whatever water is left on the surface of the clay and minimizes explosions. Another thing I do is place a little silica sand under big sculptures and flat wall pieces when I put them in the kiln. I spread out the silica sand with my hand (use a small amount); the grains act like little ball bearings and allow the piece to move as it shrinks in the kiln. This helps avoid the cracks that can occur when the clay gets stuck on something as it shrinks.

FIRING TEMPERATURES AND CLAY

There are a few different types of clay that sculptural ceramicists like to use, and they fall into categories of color, texture, and firing temperatures.

It will come as no shock to you that clay is fired to very high temperatures. Clay changes its molecular makeup at about 1000°F (538°C), and most glazes don't even melt until the kiln reaches 1800°F (982°C). Firing temperatures and the clay associated with those temperatures fall into three categories (some people might have four or more categories, but three are enough for me).

Potters refer to temperature by talking about "cones," which refers to *pyrometric cones*. These are little pyramid-shaped clay objects that are placed in the kiln with the artwork and indicate when a

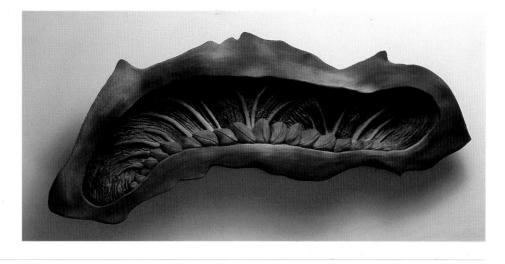

Whitney Forsyth, *Open Heart*, 1998. 27 x 13 x 6 in. (68.5 x 33 x 15.3 cm). White low-fire sculpture body with sand; slab built; fired in electric kiln, Δ04; sealed with waterproof spray paint, oil paint, clear, matte polyurethane seal.
Photo by Art Schoeby

certain clay reaches *maturity*—the point at which the clay becomes dense and glasslike. The upper range of temperatures to which a specific clay can be fired, referred to as its *cone-firing range*, is designated by the symbol Δ, followed by one or more numbers: Δ04, for example. When a specific temperature is reached, the cone softens and bends. At that point, the potter knows that the proper temperature has been reached and turns off the kiln. Many a long night has been spent waiting for Δ10 to bend.

To make things more complicated, the cone numbers are set up in a strange way. Some numbers have a zero in front of them and some don't. When they have a zero in front, the sequence is backwards: Δ06 refers to a lower temperature than Δ04! The Cone-Firing Ranges chart on page 136 helps explain the cone sequence and corresponding firing temperatures.

The important thing is to know what temperature you'll be firing to and the right words to use. Yes, even ceramic art has jargon. Say, for example, you want to arrange to have your art fired at a ceramic shop. You go in or call up and the shop person says "Okay, we'll fire it. What kind of clay is it made out of?" So, you mumble, "Uh, like, a tan-brown kind." The potter won't know what you're talking about. If, on the other hand, you write down the

clay name when you purchase it, you can respond (with a certain swagger) "It's a red stoneware clay cone 6."

Although having a working knowledge of clay is invaluable, you don't need to know everything about the nature and chemistry of clay. Just be able to identify the kind of clay you're using and what cone it fires to.

BISQUE FIRING AND MATURITY

One thing that holds true for all types of ceramicists is that clay is generally fired twice. The first time is called the *bisque firing*. This firing hardens the clay enough that you can pick it up and decorate it without breaking it. Bisque temperature is generally around Δ08 to Δ04. The second firing is to the *maturation point* of the clay; maturity, simply, means firing the clay to its recommended end point.

Firing clay to its maturation point is more relevant to ceramicists who make functional vessels, such as plates, because glazes on pottery that you intend to eat off require high firing temperatures. In ceramic sculpture, however, firing to maturity may not be such a great idea. Why? Because the clay goes through more stress as it approaches maturity—it hurts to grow! This means that a larger and more complex sculpture made in Δ6 clay might be better off being fired a bit lower, say, to Δ4—unless there

23

Left: **Liz Surbeck Biddle,** ***Angry Dog***, 1996. 10 x 14 x 6 in. (25.4 x 35.6 x 15.2 cm). Stoneware; slab built and pinched; terra sigillata, low-fire glazes, oxidation fired, Δ04. Photo by David Baer

Right: **Aurore Chabot,** ***Malaprop***, 1995. 10 x 23 x 12 in. (25.5 x 58.5 x 30.5 cm). Earthenware; press molded, reverse inlay, pinch construction; underglazes, terra sigillata slips, metallic stains; oxidation in electric kiln, Δ04. Photo by Chris Autio

is glaze on it that needs to be fired to Δ6. A clay sculptor has, in some ways, much more freedom than a potter making mugs and vases. Clay sculptors can fire clay to different temperatures than might otherwise be indicated.

Potters generalize about their ceramic work by referring to it as *low-fire, mid-fire,* or *high-fire.* The type of clay that a ceramicist uses will determine, to a large extent, the temperature at which a clay work matures after being baked in the kiln. The following is the way I identify the different clays and their firing ranges.

EARTHENWARE OR LOW-FIRE CLAYS

Earthenware or *low-fire* clays have a firing range of 1922°F to 2012°F (1050°C to 1100°C) or Δ04 to Δ02. You can purchase red or white earthenware clay. Red earthenware is sometimes called *terra cotta* which means "baked earth." It's the most common clay on earth, and the first to be used by humans to make ceramic objects. Made of decomposed rocks, organic material, and a large amount of iron, earthenware clay reaches maturity at a comparatively low temperature—such as what was achievable when our ancestors baked their pottery in simple

fire pits. Since earthenware fires at lower temperatures, the clay also tends to be somewhat porous when the piece is finished. The lower firing temperature allows you to use commercial low-fire glazes, which come in a lot of great colors. There are some wonderful, gritty red earthenware clays available that work well for sculpture. I often fire the clays higher than recommended and am able to get a deep, rich brown color from the clay.

White earthenware tends to be flabby and weak, although there are some that have silica sand and other ingredients added to make the clay stronger and give it what potters call "tooth." The advantage of working with a white clay is that glazes come out brighter and richer than they do on red clay. I like earthenware clay a lot, and think it's a good way to start making sculpture because you can get such a rich color from the clay so easily.

Note: If you choose to fire earthenware clay to Δ3 or Δ4 to get a richer color, it's important to fire a smaller test piece to be sure the particular earthenware you're using will fire that high. Usually the salesperson working at a ceramic-supply outlet will be able to help you.

MID-RANGE FIRING CLAYS

This category covers clays fired from Δ3 to Δ6. Many people consider Δ6 to be the beginning of "stoneware temperatures." As the name *stoneware* indicates, this clay is more durable, denser, and not as porous as earthenware. It's formed when rock particles mix with small particles of iron and with decayed plants containing potassium, a mineral that acts as a *flux* or melting agent.

Using a Δ6 clay and firing it to the right temperature will give you a very hard and durable sculpture. Because this is a higher temperature than earthenware, the color palette becomes more limited. This means that the pinks, yellows, and reds that are available at low temperatures become more difficult to achieve at higher temperatures.

HIGH-FIRE CLAYS

This impressive title refers to clays that are fired to Δ9 or Δ10. This is the temperature that traditional porcelain is fired to. *High-fire clays*, such as porcelain and stoneware, result in sculpture that is hard and durable. But if you're creating a complex ceramic sculpture, such as one that sits on a small or fragile base, you may be better off firing the piece at a lower temperature, perhaps to Δ8. Stoneware firings, particularly in a kiln that burns fossil fuel such as gas or wood, are great for sculptures. Salt firings, where salt is added to the kiln at peak temperature, is a spectacular way to glaze sculpture. Again we come to differences between functional pottery and sculpture. Clay sculptors don't have to glaze their work at all because they are not making items intended for holding food or water. If they do decide to glaze a piece of sculpture, they do so to bring attention to a certain area or to contrast that area with another part of the piece. When creating sculpture in clay, it's good to let the preconceived idea of glazing everything just go away. In the section called Surface Decoration (page 27), I will regale you with wonderful ways of firing and painting your work.

Left: **Lynn Wood**, *Untitled (candlestick sculpture)*, 1999. 12½ x 2 x 2 in. (31.8 x 5 x 5 cm). Porcelain; handbuilt; oxide stained, oxidation fired, Δ9. Photo by Hap Sakwa

Above: **Gerald Smith**, *Ann's Odyssey*, 1998. 18 x 17 x 13 in. (45.8 x 43.3 x 33 cm). Earthenware; wheel-thrown, press molded, slab built; glaze oxidation fired, Δ6, slips and glaze oxidation fired, Δ06. Photo by artist

PURCHASING AND PREPARING CLAY

Clay that you purchase at an art- or ceramic-supply outlet is sold in plastic bags and has been cleaned and prepared so there are no air bubbles in it. Store the clay in a heated room: you don't want it to freeze.

WEDGING CLAY

The clay that you just bought is ready to use—it's damp and free of air bubbles. But you won't always be working with fresh clay; sometimes you'll start with clay that's been sitting in a partially opened bag and has dried out a bit. Or, you may be working with clay that you've recycled or mixed yourself. You will then need to wedge the clay in order to redistribute the moisture and eliminate lumps and bubbles. Wedging makes moist clay easier to use and also gets your whole body warmed up and ready to make sculpture.

Wedge the clay on a sturdy work surface that is smooth and dry—a wooden surface is ideal. Start by pressing down on the lump of clay with the heel of one hand. Then use the other hand to slightly rotate the clay, as shown in the photo. Push and rotate the lump of clay about 20 to 40 times. Wedging is NOT like kneading bread: bread dough is folded over onto itself, which is the opposite of what you want to do with clay. When you get into the right rhythm with the clay, rocking and rotating it, a spiral pattern develops that looks like flower petals.

26

CHAPTER THREE

SURFACE DECORATION

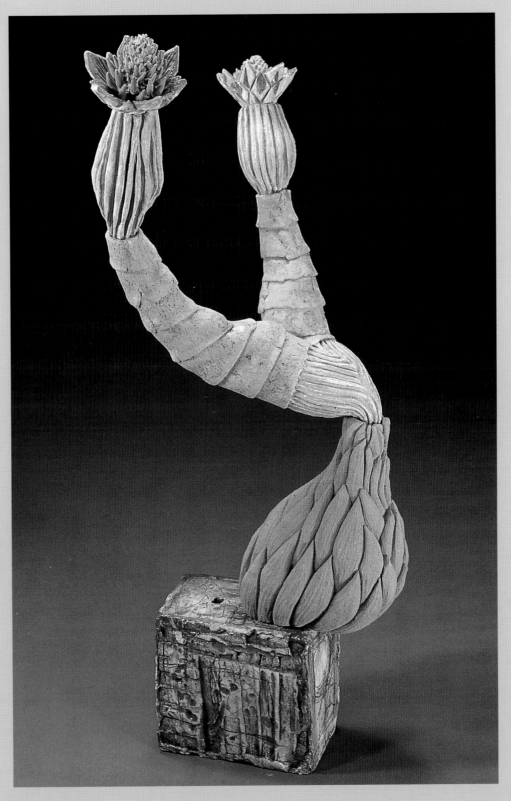

Megan Wolfe, *Reasserting Myself*, 1996. 62 x 30 x 30 in. (157.5 x 76.2 x 76.2 cm). Terra cotta; solid base, coiled additions, pinch pots, carved; bisque fired, Δ04; glaze fired Δ08 to Δ04. Photo by artist

Deborah Fleck-Stabley,
3 Candlesticks, 2000. 13 x
6 x 5 in. (33 x 15.2 x
12.7 cm). Red earthen-
ware; slab and coil built,
carved, textured; under-
glaze, glaze, special effects
glaze fired in electric kiln.
Photo by Mark Anderman

As I MENTIONED IN the previous sections, ceramics can be a technical and confusing business. There are so many different clays, glazes, firing techniques, and decorating methods to learn about. Keep in mind that many of those techniques apply mainly to pottery, such as plates, mugs, and vases, which must be glazed to make them waterproof or safe and appealing to use with food.

For nonfunctional ceramic sculpture, I favor simple finishing techniques and am not adverse to nontraditional finishes, such as paints, wood stains, or shoe polish. An old friend of mine used to call these finishes "RTG" for "room temperature glazes." There are many potters who frown on these finishes, but I think they're fine if they accomplish your goal. Therein lies the rub: you need to have a goal, a way that you want your piece to look.

IDENTIFYING THE ARTIST WITHIN

How do you get to that place? By making many ceramic pieces and finishing them in a number of different ways. By looking at your work, not as a single "product," but as part of a long road, a process in which you create art from clay on a regular basis in order to learn about clay and about yourself. If you're able to do this (and carving out this kind of time isn't easy, given how hectic contemporary life can be) what will happen is that the "product," the individual artwork, will, over time, improve dramatically. You will reap the benefits of a beautiful, fulfilling activity without worrying about "productivity," without asking yourself in a negative way, "what am I doing?" and without thinking, "it should look like that person's work."

It isn't easy to remove years of anxiety about your artistic ability. Many people, including you, have had a hand in stifling that ability, and it will take time to recover. If you observe three to four-year-old kids in a classroom making art, you'll notice that they're footloose and open, making wonderful pieces with perfect composition and color combinations. But if you watch a group of 11 and 12 year olds, you'll see how rigid, self-conscious, and confused most have become about making art.

So it's up to you to keep things simple, nonjudgmental, and enjoyable in order to find your way back. Here, then, are some simple firing and finishing techniques, some of which are nontraditional.

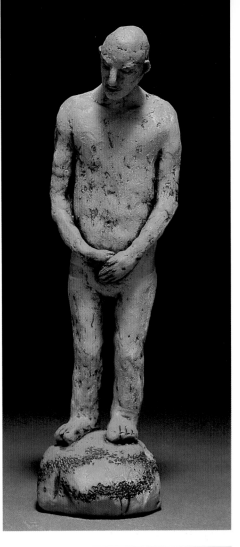

Above: **Pam Arena**, *There was an Old Lady who Lived...*, 1999. 8 x 10 x 3 in. (20.3 x 25.4 x 7.6 cm). Terra cotta; slab built; velvet underglazes; embellished with rusted wire; fired in electric kiln, Δ04. Photo by Mike Noa

Right: **Bonnie Baer**, *Man in Thought*, 1999. 15 x 4½ x 3½ in. (37.5 x 11.3 x 8.8 cm). Low-fire earthenware; handbuilt; textured with found objects; stained with oxides, Δ04. Photo by Michael Noa

TRADITIONAL SURFACES

Traditional surface applications for decorating ceramics are comprised of ingredients that react to drying and the heat of the kiln in specific ways. For that reason, they serve different purposes, and each is usually applied to the clay piece in a particular sequence to achieve a certain effect. I encourage you to experiment and break the "rules" in order to achieve the effects you want, or simply, to find out what is possible.

SLIPS, UNDERGLAZES, AND ENGOBES

Nowadays the terms *underglazes*, *slips*, and *engobes* are used nearly interchangeably. Back in the Stone Age when I started working with clay, people made a big deal out of the differences (and there are some) between these products. It's not important to get too hung up on these definitions for the purposes of this book.

Essentially a *slip* is a finely sieved mixture of clay and water that can be applied to clay surfaces in one or more layers. Slips are used to attach clay pieces together when building sculpture. They are also applied to create a neutral ground on which to apply other surface decorations. You can make a slip from the clay body you're using for the sculpture, add a ceramic colorant (oxides or ceramic stains), and wind up with a colored slip that you can paint on the clay. Colored slips are meant to be applied to clay that is in the damp or leather hard stage. Because they're made from the clay, slip glazes match the clay body to which you apply them, which means that the clay in the glaze shrinks at the same rate as the base clay.

An *underglaze*, in the most general terms, is any coloring material used under a glaze. This definition is now used to describe commercially made products colored with oxides and stains, formulated

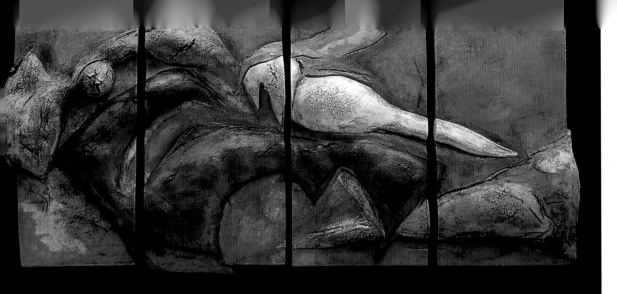

Gayle Tustin, *Three Muses*, 1998. 18 x 40 x 4 in. (45.7 x 101.6 x 10.2 cm). Red earthenware; hand-built with slabs and coils, carved; terra sigillata fired, Δ06. Patinas, bisqued terra sigillata and refired, Δ03. Photo by artist

to color greenware and bisqueware before a glaze is applied. These underglazes contain fillers, binders, and other chemicals that keep the coloring materials in suspension and minimize shrinkage.

Engobes are similar to slips, but contain binders and melting agents to make them melt and make sure they shrink to fit the clay body to which they're applied. They are designed to be painted on greenware or bisqueware and then fired.

Generally speaking, underglazes, slips, and engobes are designed to be put on the clay, fired, and then—according to what you hope to achieve—covered with a glaze. This makes them all, technically, underglazes because they're all applied underneath a glaze. The important difference is that, generally, a slip is made from the same clay the artwork is made from, which means you need to apply it before the clay dries too much; otherwise, when the piece shrinks, the slip might not "fit" and will peel off. Engobes are mixed with shrinkage compatibility in mind; there are formulas for engobes to use on damp, leather-hard, and bone-dry clay.

Ceramicists who make functional pottery almost always cover a slip with glaze: it's much nicer to eat off a glazed surface than a dry, scratchy slip-surface. Ceramicists like us, who make sculpture that no one will eat from, are free to use slips, engobes, and underglazes in any way we want. Best of all, we can buy underglazes in all sorts of colors from a ceramic-supply house or we can

mix simple ones ourselves. I use these products in my sculpture sparingly and only in keeping with the form of the work.

TERRA SIGILATTA

Terra sigilatta (sealed earth), often referred to in potter's jargon as "terra sig," is a thin variety of slip, produced by mixing powdered clay with water and a *deflocculant* (a material that eases the attraction between clay particles, allowing the mixture to flow); then the mixture is allowed to settle for 24 hours. The potter uses the finest particles of this mixture (the coarse particles settle to the bottom) to paint on the piece. Terra sig can be brushed, sponged, sprayed, dipped, or poured in a thin coat onto bone-dry greenware, the dryness stage at which it most readily adheres. Terra sig was used by the Greeks and Romans to seal and decorate their clay works. It's a good choice for sculpture because it's not glassy or shiny; instead terra sig has a soft, satin quality when polished that looks wonderful on sculpture.

You can buy terra sigilatta ready-made or you can make your own. (I have included a preparation method and formula in the appendix on page 135.) It takes a lot of time to make this mixture, so feel free to buy it. If you choose to smoke-fire your work (see page 79), a white terra sig will help achieve really dark areas, whereas red terra sig will resist some of the smoke and give rich orange and red results.

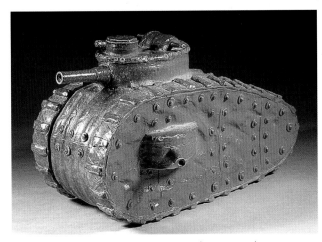

Michael J. Knox, II, *Vintage Toys*, 15½ x 11 x 9½ in. (39.5 x 28 x 24 cm). Stoneware; slab built, wheel-thrown and altered forms, hollow construction; salt-fired, Δ10.

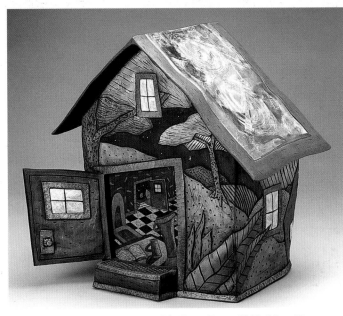

David Stabley, *House Form with Open Door*, 1999. 20 x 19 x 12 in. (50.8 x 48.3 x 30.5 cm). Red earthenware; slab built, low-relief carved; wax patina, drawing on hardboard, roof is paper collage; fired in electric kiln, Δ05. Photo by Mark Anderman

GLAZES

No discussion of ceramics would be complete without mentioning glazes, a subject that can fill a whole book. *Glazes* are mixtures of ingredients that create a glasslike covering on the clay after it's fired. A glaze can be shiny or matte, textured or glossy. It can be transparent or opaque, richly pigmented or solid black. Glazes are similar to clay in terms of chemical composition; in fact, clay is an ingredient in almost all glaze recipes. There are hundreds of glaze formulations, but all of them contain three essential components: *silica*, also called *flint*, which melts at around 3100°F (1710°C); *fluxes*, compounds that combine with silica to make it melt at a lower temperature; and *alumina*, a refractory element that makes the glaze stronger and harder, and prevents excessive running. Other ingredients, including coloring oxides and stains, and fluxes that are compatible with various firing temperatures, result in different glazing effects.

Glazes are usually applied to bisque-fired work, and the glazed piece is then fired again to melt the glaze. Glazes are grouped into low-fire, medium-fire, and high-fire temperatures. Ceramic suppliers sell many prepared glazes for all three categories. In the bibliography (page 143), I list several books that explain the use of glazes in detail.

In the hands of someone with a great deal of experience, a glaze can be used to great advantage on ceramic sculpture. It also can destroy a piece of sculpture by focusing all the attention on a glossy colored surface at the expense of the form that you have worked so hard to capture. A word of caution and encouragement: Although glazes are frequently used by potters, you don't have to glaze your sculpture. You do probably want to apply some kind of a finish to the work, but even that is not absolutely necessary. Some clay bodies look so great when they're fired in a reduction atmosphere to maturing temperature that they need nothing at all. That is why I emphasize working on the form of your sculpture so that it becomes the focal point.

CERAMIC STAINS

The same pigments used to make glazes, engobes, and colored slips, can be used alone with a little water to add color to ceramic sculpture—these mixtures are called *ceramic stains* or *stains*. Raw ceramic pigments are the metallic elements of the earth. Some of the most commonly used are iron oxide, cobalt oxide, and copper oxide. Cobalt and copper also can be purchased in the carbonate form—copper carbonate and cobalt carbonate. The oxide form of the pigment is stronger and

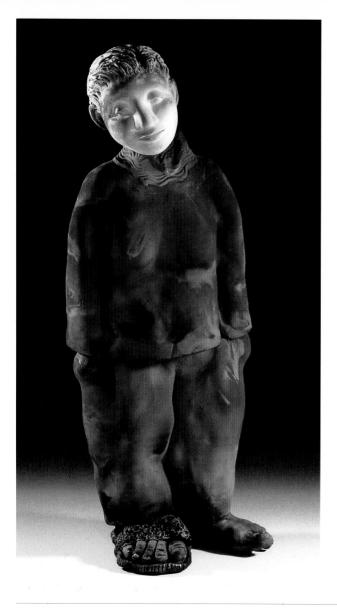

Above: **Renée Azenaro**, *Purple Moon Rising*, 1989. 18 x 15 x 24 inches (46 x 38 x 61 cm). White stoneware; slab built; glaze; stains, oxides; oxidation fired, Δ5. Photo by artist

Left: **Judy Geerts**, *My Father Had Alzheimers Disease. Will I?*, 1999. 21 x 8 x 6 in. (52.5 x 20 x 15 cm). White raku clay; body slab built; head and feet pinched, detailed; scarf textured with corrugated cardboard; bisque fired, Δ04; glaze fired in electric kiln, Δ05; copper matte raku with newspaper and sawdust reduction, Δ07. Photo by Larry Dikeman

harder to disperse in water than the carbonate form. These pigments can be mixed into water, stirred thoroughly (they settle quickly), and applied to a bisqued sculpture. They contain no clay or melting agents, (although you could add some, thereby creating an engobe or slip!) so their effect is matte, with strong natural colors, especially in the case of red iron oxide—my favorite and the favorite of millions.

Although beautiful colored stains in many hues are commercially available, I think a simple, iron oxide stain is a good starting place to learn about finishing sculpture. I texture a piece while it's leather hard, and bisque fire it. With a brush, I wash over the piece with the stain. I wait for the stain to dry a bit; then I sponge off the top layer of pigment, and in so doing, leave some pigment in the recesses. (I clean the sponge after every wipe.) This gives the piece great contrast and emphasizes the texture I gave it.

Once I taught a class in Central America as a visiting artist. This particular school had little in the way of tools or equipment for ceramics. In order to finish our pieces, we scraped rust off iron scraps, and mixed it with water—that's what iron oxide is—just rust. Traveling and teaching in different countries has helped me appreciate simplicity in making and finishing ceramic artwork. Yes, there are commercial ceramic pigments available in a rainbow of colors. I urge you to ask yourself: What does my piece need? Then be open to following the simple road, keeping in mind that "simple" and "easy" are not necessarily the same thing.

Ravit Lazer, *Untitled*, 1998. 10 x 6 x 4 to 21½ x 10 x 10 in. (25 x 15 x 10 cm to 55 x 25 x 25 cm). Stoneware; slab built, textured; washed, sponged with oxides, glazes oxidation fired, Δ9. Photo by Soho Photographer

NONTRADITIONAL SURFACES

Here we enter into the realm of nonfired finishes. I would recommend learning how to use traditional finishes before trying these out. Try these finishes on scrap clay or small test pieces before putting them on your sculpture.

These finishes require you to look at your work in a different way: it is now a sculpture and can be treated with unusual or nonceramic finishes. These finishes are applied only to bisque or mature clay! The piece needs to be able to withstand water and rubbing. Some of these finishes can be applied to clay that has been fired to its maturity, and some depend on the clay still being a little porous. Try firing your piece a cone or two under its maturation point to retain some porosity.

OIL AND ACRYLIC PAINT

I have used both oil and acrylic paints on ceramic sculpture. Oil paint looks good on stoneware, but it takes a long time to dry. Acrylic paint, on the other hand, drys quickly but doesn't look as rich as oil—it is, after all, plastic! Either way, the point is not so much what you use but how you use it. If you simply squeeze out some paint and coat your sculpture with it, you can be relatively sure you will make a horror of it. Why? Because you will cover the intrinsic beauty of the clay itself. If, instead, you use the paint as an accent, or rub it in and then wipe off the top surface, you will be working with the artwork and not against it.

If you use oil paints, you will need turpentine as a paint thinner and a cleaner for your brushes. These things give off fumes, so be sure your work area is well ventilated. If you use a lot of thinner, open a window. Be sure to dispose of your thinner and rags in an environmentally responsible way. Acrylic paints clean up with soap and water, and go on easily. Again be careful with the application of the paint—don't just coat the whole piece. I like to use the darker pigments, such as red iron, umber, and burnt sienna. I brush on small amounts, use a rag or an old paintbrush to work it into the surface, and then quickly wipe it off to gauge its effect. I have also used a propane torch to partially burn the oil or acrylic paint, and then wiped it off. I would not recommend using a torch if you have turpentine or any other flammable liquid around, or you may quickly start a fire! I mention the torch mainly to demonstrate how creative thinking can be applied to using your tools.

Kelly Connole, *Embracing Alice*, 1999.
74 x 84 x 108 in. (188 x 213.3 x 274.3
cm). Δ6 sculpture clay; figure built solid,
hollowed from behind when leather
hard; *Proud Brown Rabbit*, 1999, 29 x
14 x 20 in. (73.8 x 35.5 x 50.8 cm) and
Leery White Rabbit, 1999, 19 x 12 x 21
in. (48.3 x 30.5 x 53.3 cm). Δ6 sculpture body; coil built, appendages added
when soft-leather hard, carved;
engobes, glazes, underglazes fired in
electric kiln, Δ6. Photo by artist

WOOD STAINS AND WAX SHOE POLISH

Using wood stain and shoe polish on clay sculpture
is truly unconventional. As a sculptor I am accus-
tomed to seeking out any kind of finish for my
work since I work in plaster, wood, metal, stone,
and with found objects. As a result, I approach
ceramic sculpture in much the same way. The difference is that I have great respect and love for the
material itself—the clay. I try not to cover it up or
to make it look like something else: I try to work
with it. Wood finishes come in a vast array of colors and formulas. Again, I tend to favor the darker
stains, such as walnut. I brush the stain onto a

couple of small areas at a time, and then dab at
those areas with a clean rag. You need to wait until
the stain is dry to really know how it will look;
these products work better on porous or semiporous surfaces. Once the stain is dry, you can sand
a little off to reveal the clay.

Wax shoe polish is a mixture of wax, turpentine,
and pigment. It also works better on porous or
semiporous surfaces. I rub it on with a soft rag and
wipe it off right away. Remember to work slowly,
and keep in mind the natural beauty of the clay.
Work with it.

CHAPTER FOUR

THE PROJECTS

The seven projects in this chapter were designed to offer instruction on the hollow-form sculpture techniques that are the focus of this book— coil, slab, and pinch. Most use combinations of all three techniques. All the projects are appropriate for beginners, and are arranged in an order that encourages you to build upon the skills you are learning. Some are quite representational; others less so. Enjoy them for their own sake. Then, let them inspire you to create your own forms.

CAT AT REST

This is a particularly good project for beginners. To simplify the form, the cat is in a resting position with its feet pulled in—maybe it's recovering from chasing a mouse. The sculpture is streamlined down to its essential parts, relying for emphasis on the cat's distinctive facial features. When you make this cat, you'll learn quite a bit about making a strong, overall form and about how to sculpt (also called model) the features of a face.

MATERIALS AND TOOLS

Clay

Wooden dowels in various sizes, ranging from ½ inch to 2 inches (1.3 to 5 cm) wide★

Newspaper

Wooden paddle

Epsom salts and slip mixture (see page 17)

Paintbrushes

Serrated rib

Rubber and wooden ribs

Wooden modeling tools in various sizes and shapes

Ribbon tool

Pin tool

Turntable

Soft sponge

Brown commercial glaze

Iron oxide stain

★available at hardware and building-supply stores

SHAPING THE BODY

1 Start with a lump of clay large enough to represent a full-grown cat. Wedge the clay thoroughly. It's important to get out all the air bubbles and to get the clay and your hands ready for work.

2 With your hands, shape the clay into a slight cone shape, wider at one end than the other.

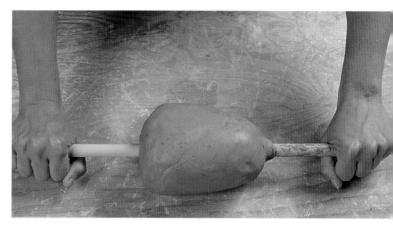

3 Carefully push the thinnest dowel through the center of the form. To open the clay, repeat using increasingly wider dowels.

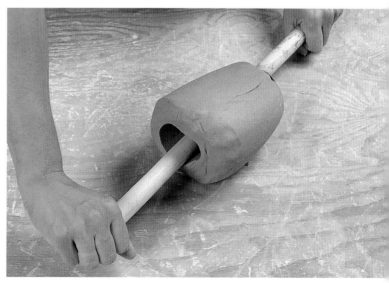

4 Grasp each end of the dowel and slowly roll the clay. With a little practice, you can control the

shape and thickness of the clay. By switching to a thicker dowel, you can make the clay even thinner.

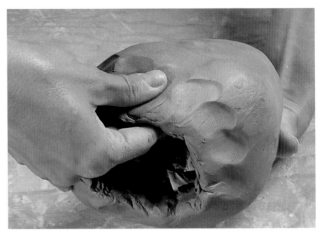

you take your work somewhere to be fired, be sure to tell them that there is paper inside.

5 Set the dowel aside and pick up the form so that the narrow end is facing you.

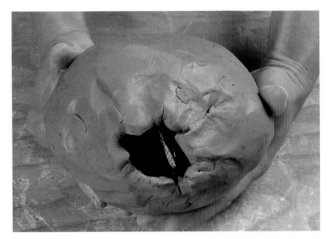

7 Turn the form over so that the wide end is facing you, and pinch and squeeze the clay towards the inside to begin closing the hole.

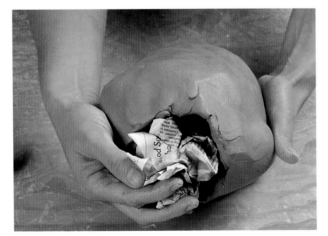

6 Crumple up some sheets of newspaper, and push them into the form. Use enough paper so that the form feels pretty full; the idea is to give the form support from the inside. Don't worry about the paper—it will burn out in the firing. If

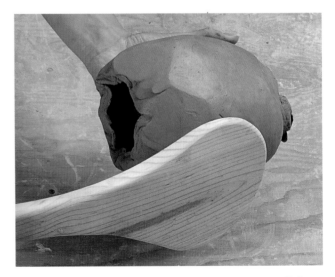

8 Use the wooden paddle to help close off the form. Paddling the clay stretches it and shapes it. Paddle lightly with long strokes along the sides

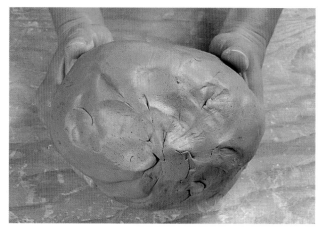

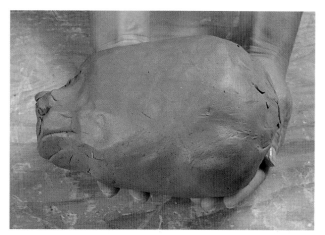

and top of the form. The idea is to stretch the clay at the top and close it off; try not to hit the clay from above and hammer it shut—this will change the form, which you don't want to do. Here's what the wide end should look like after it's completely closed off.

10 Repeat this on the other side; try to line up the leg shapes so they're more or less at the same place on either side of the body. You may want to lay the form down and draw a faint line from top to bottom to indicate where the spine would be; this can help keep things symmetrical.

SHAPING THE HEAD

1 Roll out a round ball of clay that will become the cat's head. Notice the size of the ball in photo 14 in relation to the body: if you made a few balls and laid them end to end, how many would it take to be as long as the body? This is one method for estimating the relationship, in size, of one form to another, also known as proportion. When parts relate to one another well, the whole form looks "right." Try to get the proportion of the head to the body "right." But don't worry too much because clay at this stage is soft, and it's easy to change the size of the head.

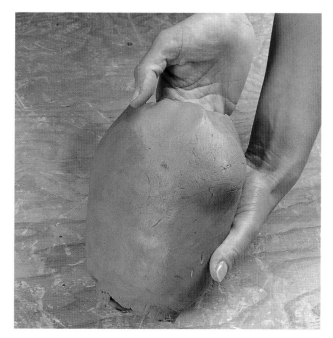

9 Turn the form so that the side faces you and lightly run your finger along the side to trace the shape of the leg; it should look like a small oval. Trace this shape lightly, until you're satisfied with the placement and shape. Then reach inside the form and push the oval shape outward with your fingers by stroking them against the clay lightly, pushing a little harder each time until the shape of the haunch emerges.

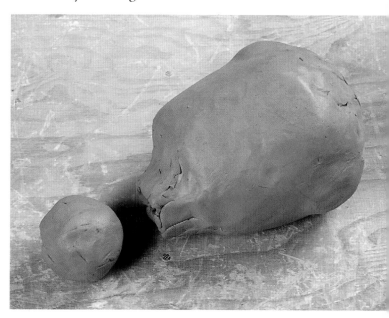

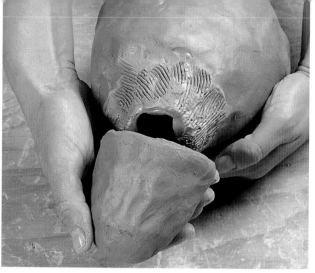

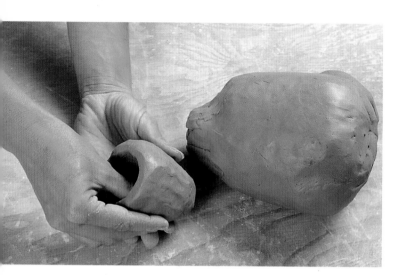

2 Make a small pinch pot out of the clay ball (and set it aside; this will become the cat's head.

 5 Slip the wide end of the head onto the body.

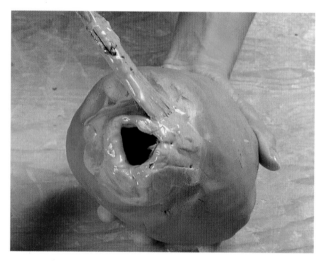

3 Brush slip onto the narrow end of the cat's body.

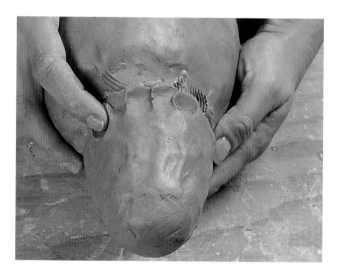

6 Use your thumb to firmly attach the head to the body. Be sure to use the pin tool to make a few small pinholes in the body of the cat and in the head to release trapped air. This is very important; failure to do this could lead to the piece exploding in the kiln.

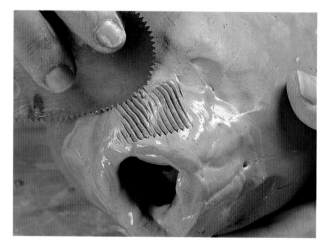

4 Use the serrated rib to thoroughly score the narrow end of the body around the opening. Score the inside of the cat's head, too.

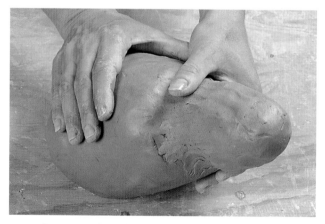

7 Squeeze the clay gently to form a slight neck. Try not to exaggerate the neck or make it seem too rigid or stiff.

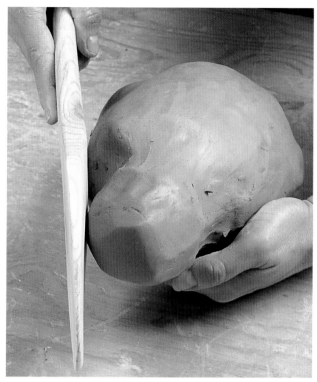

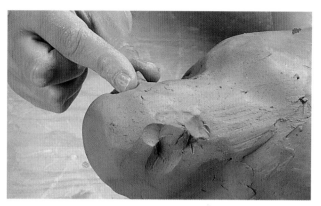

2 Reach back along the sides of the head and grab a little clay. Pinch it out and form it into a small triangle, then into an ear. Turn the head so it faces you, and create another ear on the other side.

8 Paddle the head into a slightly conical form.

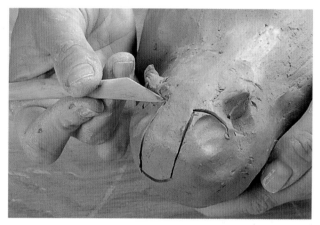

MODELING THE HEAD AND FACE

1 To begin shaping the head and face, place your finger on what will be the tip of the nose, and sweep it back towards the cat's neck; this will create a flat plane and start to differentiate the parts of the face. The cat will have a broad nose area; the nose itself will be a triangle at the end of a rectangle, which ends where the eyes begin.

3 Use the pointed end of a wooden modeling tool to draw a long rectangle down the center of the cat's face, with a triangle at the end where the nose will be, and curved lines at the other end in the shape of eyebrow ridges.

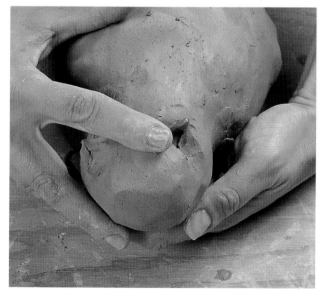

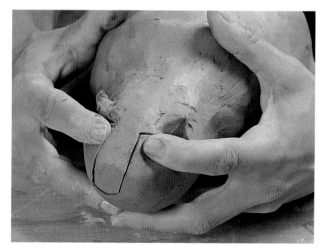

4 Place your fingers where the eyebrow lines end, and dig deeply in the clay with each fingertip to make small eye cavities.

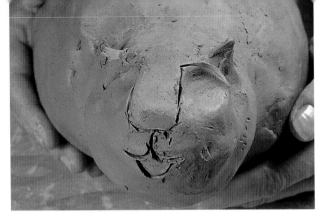

5 Use a modeling tool to shape the eye cavities and model the area around them. Don't worry too much about detail; we'll come back and work on them more later. Use the modeling stick to draw in the shape of the mouth.

6 The photo above shows how the head, mouth, eyes, and ears should look at this stage in terms of proportion. Yours will look different because it is yours. Don't be afraid to deviate from this example, and change the shape of the eyes or ears. Experiment and enjoy the sensation of sculpting clay.

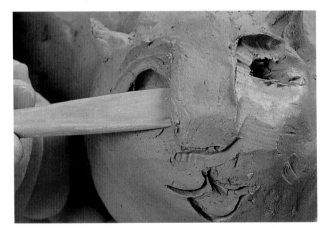

7 Use the modeling stick to push down along the sides of the nose to give form to it. Do the same along the eyes to make them into a flat plane raised up from the body.

8 Brush slip on the areas around the base of the ears and the eyes. We will soon add clay to build up mass in these facial areas.

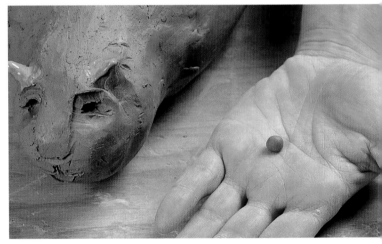

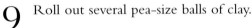

9 Roll out several pea-size balls of clay.

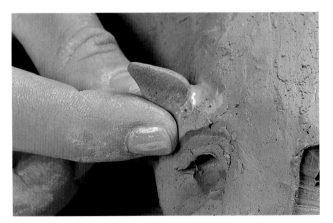

10 Add these pieces to the base of the ears and to the area just above the eyes to build up the brow. While we let this area stiffen up, we will turn our attention to sculpting the feet, which are partially tucked under the cat's body.

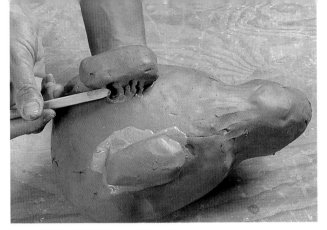

11 Roll out four teardrop-shaped pieces of clay about 2½ inches (6.3 cm) in length. Each piece will be one foot of the cat, so try and make them all about the same size. Turn the cat over, slip and score the underside carefully, and attach the two back feet.

12 Attach the front feet. The feet should start out right from the end of the oval haunch form, all four making a sort of "L" form. There's no need to show too much of the foot.

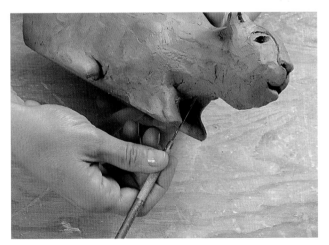

13 Use the pin tool to make a few small pin-holes in the body of the cat and in the head to release trapped air. This is very important; failure to do this could lead to the piece exploding in the kiln.

14 Place the cat on the turntable that is covered with newspaper or scrap paper. Roll out several more pea-size balls of clay. Push these small pieces onto the face to add mass to the different parts; blend the little balls to make them fit the cat's face. In this way you can slowly build up facial areas and give them prominence, especially along the mouth and chin.

15 To add relief and detail to the face, use the ribbon tool to remove some clay from the eyes. Use a modeling tool to model the whiskers. As the clay stiffens, it will be easier to add sharper detail.

COMPLETING THE BODY

1 Use the rubber rib to smooth down the body.

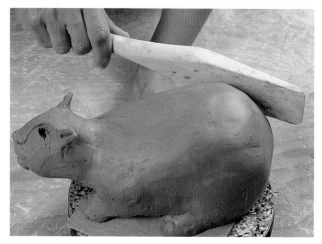

2 To gently shape the cat's body and the area around the feet, use the wooden paddle.

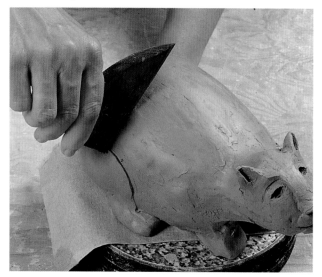

3 Use the wooden rib to indent and outline the shape of the rear haunch of the cat.

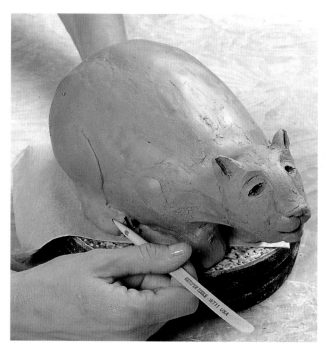

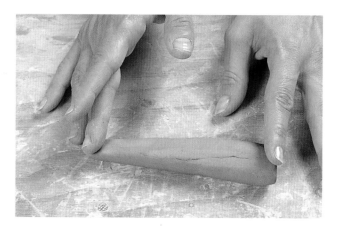

4 With a wooden modeling stick, make three lines in the feet to represent toes.

5 For the tail, roll out a thick coil, tapering it by rolling it and pressing more on one end.

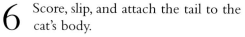

6 Score, slip, and attach the tail to the cat's body.

FINISHING THE CAT SCULPTURE

1 Let the cat dry slowly under plastic. Sometimes I uncover a sculpture for a few hours and then cover it up again for a few so that it can dry slowly. But don't let the sculpture dry too fast by leaving it uncovered for a long time. The tail and other parts might dry more quickly than the body, and crack as a result.

2 Bisque fire the cat to Δ06.

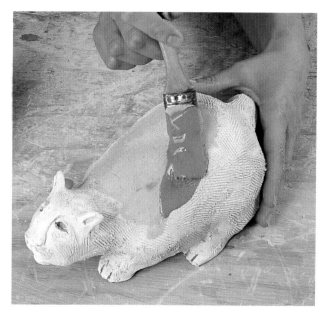

3 Brush two coats of brown commercial glaze on the cat's body, but not on the face—we don't want to obscure the cat's features. The glaze appears gray because it hasn't been fired yet. When the glaze is dry, paint red iron oxide stain on top of the glaze, being sure to cover the cat's face. Let that dry, then use a wet sponge to remove most of the glaze from the body, leaving some in the textured areas of the body. Don't remove the iron oxide stain from the face.

4 Fire the piece to Δ6 in an electric kiln.

7 Texture the sculpture heavily with a serrated rib.

BIRD ON A
TREE PEDESTAL

*Birds, like fish, have streamlined bodies. We are
used to seeing birds in flight, so capturing them
in a heavy medium such as clay is a challenge.
In this piece we learn the relationship between
the head and the body of the bird, and make a
base that is part of the sculpture. After you complete this project, spend some
time observing birds in flight
and at rest to learn more
about their form. Then make
a different type of bird.*

MATERIALS AND TOOLS

Clay

Newspaper

Pin tool

Wooden modeling tools in various sizes
and shapes

Epsom salts and slip mixture (see page 17)

Paintbrushes

Serrated rib

Iron oxide stain

Blue commercial glaze

SHAPING THE BODY

1 Roll out a ball of prepared clay that is slightly
narrower at one end. Insert your thumb into
the wider end, and pinch the clay in your fingers,
turning it as you go. In this way, you will create a
hollow cylindrical form.

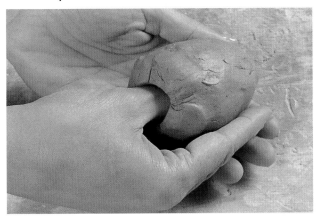

2 Insert a sheet of bunched up newspaper into
the form.

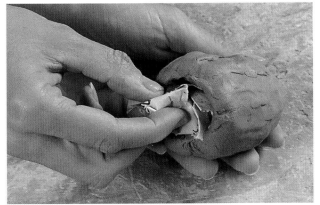

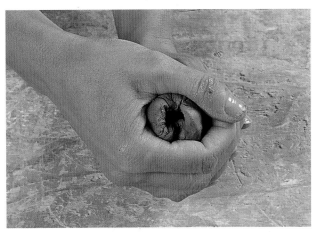

3 Pinch and squeeze the form closed. Remember
to pierce the body with a pin tool to allow
air to escape; if you don't do this, the piece could
crack or explode in the firing.

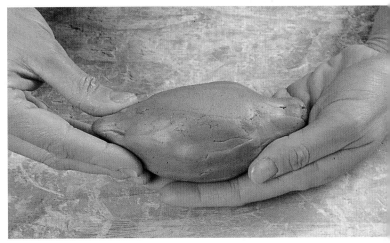

4 Smooth the clay with your fingers, and
stretch it slightly to form a shape like a
lemon. This will be the start of the bird's face.

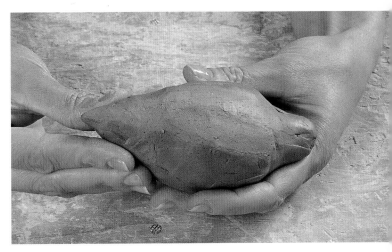

5 Dampen your fingers with a little water and
begin to stroke and pull out the beak.

6 Use a pointed-end modeling tool to define the beak and eyes.

7 Using a slant-edge modeling tool, mark the location of the wings on both sides of the bird's body.

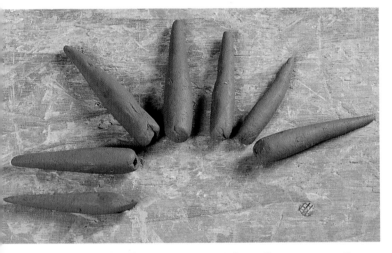

8 Roll out seven to eight coils to use as tail and wing parts. Those pictured in photo 8 are about 2 to 3 inches (5.1 to 7.6 cm) long. Make two of them slightly larger than the rest. Notice that the coils taper down to a thin end; this is important because the shape helps to emphasize movement when you apply them to the bird's body.

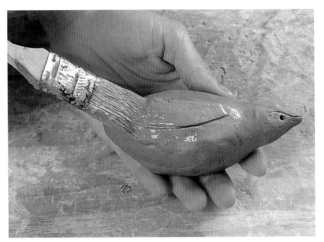

9 Coat the wing area on both sides of the body with slip.

10 Using one of the larger coils, press the wider end down on the body to secure it in place. Make sure you have the wing oriented in the right direction!

11 Add a smaller coil above the first one. Repeat this process with a large and small coil on the other side of the body.

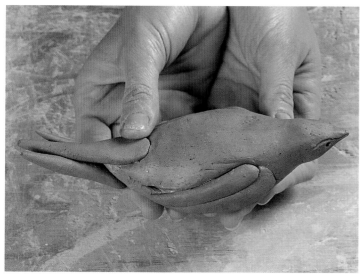

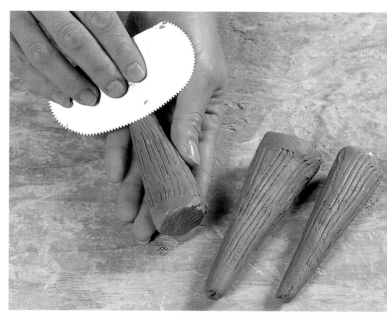

12 Coat the bird's tail end with slip, and attach the three tail pieces. Be sure to smooth the wider ends that attach to the body. I like to leave the coil ends intact—I don't smooth them so much that they integrate into the body.

MAKING THE TREE PEDESTAL

1 Form a disk shape and pound it flat. This will be the base of the pedestal, so it needs to be flat and a little thick, about ⅜ of an inch (9.5 mm), and just slightly larger that the bird itself. The size of the base is important. If it's too small, the sculpture might not sit right and could topple over; if it's too large, it will dwarf the sculpture.

2 Form three cone shapes by rolling out thick coils and tapering them. Use a serrated rib to apply a vertical texture to the coils; this will help emphasize movement. Again, the size of the coils is important. If you wish to emphasize the bird, then make the coils about 1 inch shorter in length than the bird; if you wish to make the bird appear smaller and emphasize the base, then make the coils 2 to 3 inches (5.1 to 7.6 cm) longer than the bird.

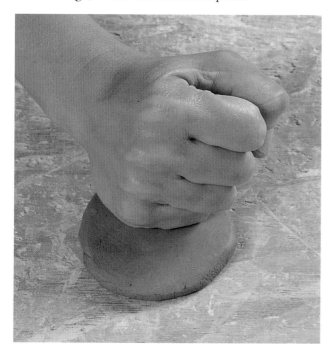

3 Apply slip to the inside edges of the base coils and press them together.

4 Twist and weave the coils together to create a treelike form.

5 Slip and score the base and the ends of the coils; then attach the tree form securely to the base.

FINISHING THE BIRD AND PEDESTAL

1 Cover the sculpture with plastic and let it dry slowly.

2 When the sculpture is dry, bisque fire it to Δ06.

3 Paint the bisque-fired base with an iron oxide stain; apply one thick coat, and when it's dry, rub it off with a sponge, leaving pigment in the recesses of the textured base.

4 Apply a coat of blue glaze to the bird's body, let it dry, and then rub it off in places.

5 Fire the bird to Δ6 in an electric kiln.

6 Slip and score the body of the bird. Attach the body securely to the tree form, turning the bird in a direction that you find pleasing.

BIRD-HUMAN CREATURE

In this project we add some distinctly human qualities to a version of the bird sculpture to create a mythological winged figure. This is a great way to stretch your creativity and have fun with the material. Keep in mind that as long as you attach the clay well and follow good techniques in constructing your sculpture, there is no limit to the kinds of things you can make. Feel free to add more coils or make up your own types of forms as you work on this project.

MATERIALS AND TOOLS

Clay

Newspaper

Pin tool

Wooden modeling tools in various sizes
and shapes

Epsom salts and slip mixture (see page 17)

Paintbrushes

Serrated rib

Iron oxide stain

Soft sponge

Commercial turquoise glaze

SHAPING THE BODY AND HEAD

1 Roll out an egg-shaped mound of clay. Make a pinch pot by inserting your thumb into the form and pinching the clay upwards while turning it in your hands. Insert bunched up newspaper into the form, and squeeze the hole closed. (Refer to the Bird on a Tree Pedestal, steps 2 and 3 on page 47, for more details.) Be sure to pierce the body with a pin tool in various places to release air; if you don't do this, your piece could crack or explode in the kiln.

2 Smooth the end of the bird form with your hands.

3 Lightly choke one end to create a separation between the head and the body.

4 Push into the head with your fingers to create the eye cavities.

5 Use your fingers to draw out some clay and shape the face.

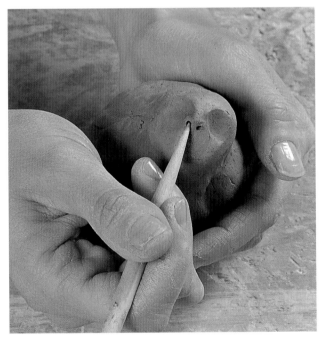

6 Create nostrils, using the pointed-end modeling tool.

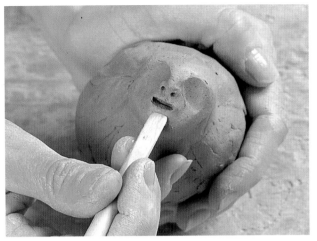

7 Use a blunt-end modeling tool to create the opening for the mouth.

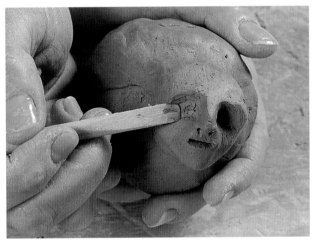

8 Use the modeling tools to create the brow ridge and the eye holes.

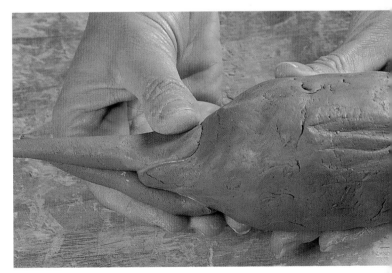

9 Form two long coils; these will be the main tail feathers. Coat the end of the body with slip and attach the coils, overlapping them slightly.

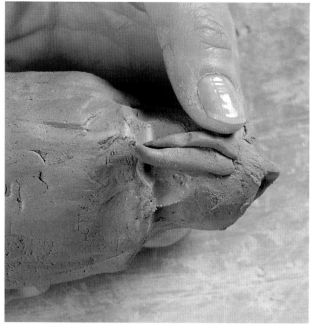

10 Roll out 8 to 10 smaller, thinner coils, and attach them to the head to create feathers.

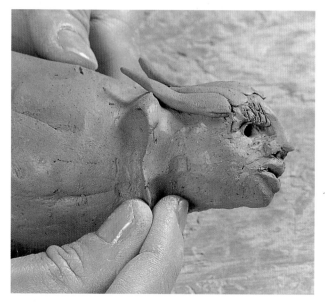

11 Pinch out the clay around the neck to create further separation from the body.

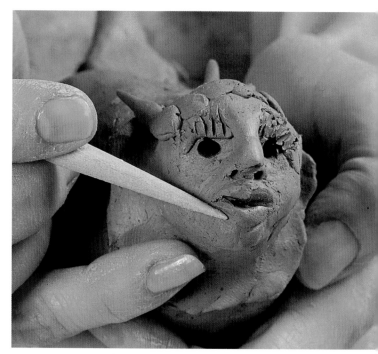

12 Using tiny coils and small bits of clay, model the mouth and lips. Complete the eyes and nose by pressing small pieces of clay in place with your modeling tool. Remember to use fresh, soft clay for this part.

CREATING THE WINGS

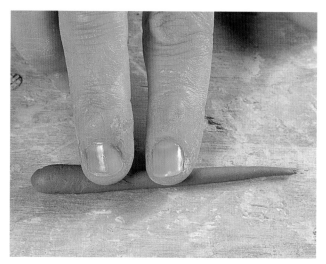

1 Roll out six to eight coils about 2 to 3 inches (5.1 to 7.6 cm) long. Remember to taper them. You will use these to embellish the wing and tail feathers.

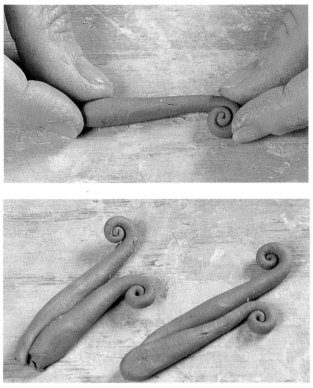

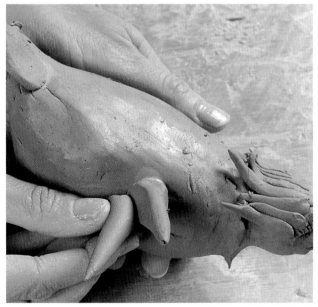

2 Dampen the coils slightly with water, and roll the ends up. Put them in sets of two and set them aside.

3 For the wing feathers, roll out 10 to 15 coils and shape them into various-size cone shapes. Take four shapes of similar size, score and slip the bottoms, and attach two on each side of the body.

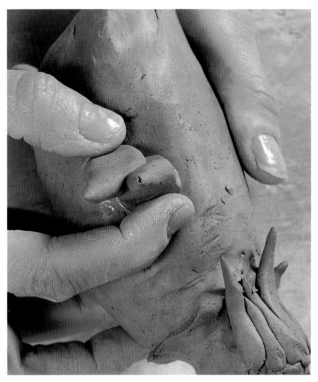

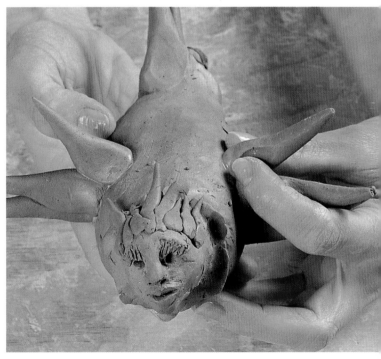

4 Pinch the forms slightly against one another, and press them forward to create a sense of movement.

5 Add two more wing feathers on each side, pressing and pinching as before.

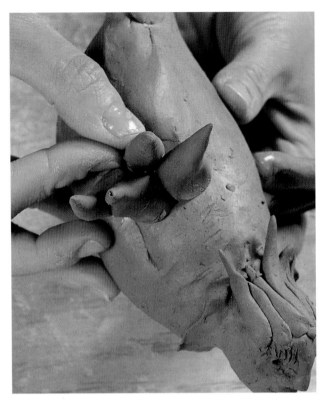

6 You should now have four coils as wings on both sides of the body.

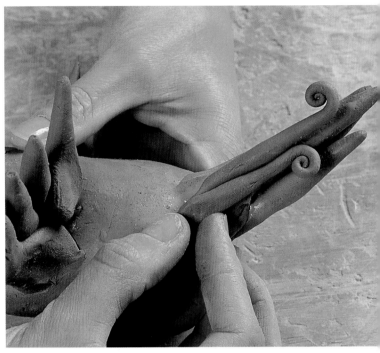

8 Attach a few of the small, rolled coils to the tail feathers, using slip to secure them in place.

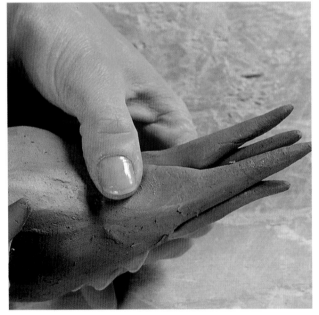

7 Fill out the tail by attaching two or more small coils to the end of the body; be sure to coat the area first with slip and smooth the end where you have attached them.

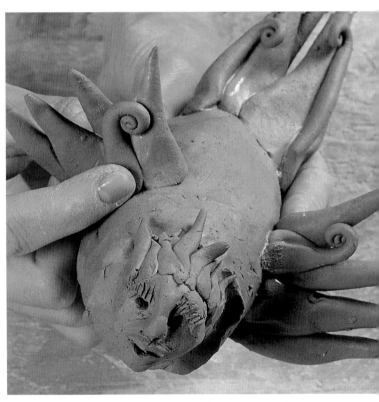

9 Attach a few rolled coils to the wings in the same manner.

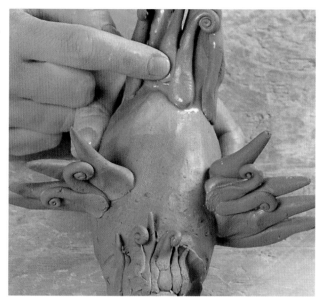

10 Attach a few small rolled coils to the head and the tail.

MAKING THE PEDESTAL BASE

1 Create the base as demonstrated in the bird project (steps 1 to 6 on pages 49 to 50). Press the figure onto the base. Since this creature might be a little heavy, you can wait awhile for the pedestal to stiffen up sufficiently for it to support the weight of the sculpture.

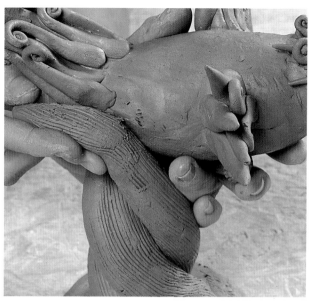

2 Be sure the figure is well balanced on the base.

FINISHING THE SCULPTURE

1 Let the piece dry under plastic for a few days and then uncover it.

2 When it's dry, bisque fire it to Δ06.

3 Dilute the iron oxide stain with a little water to create a wash; then apply it to the body and base. While it's still wet, rub some of the wash off the body with a wet sponge. Let dry.

4 For contrast, use a paintbrush to apply differ-ent layers of turquoise glaze on the tail and wings, leaving the body with just the red iron stain.

5 Fire the sculpture to Δ6 in an electric kiln.

THE FISH

This whimsical fish project is a great exercise in learning how to give the appearance of movement to a sculpture. You will also see how to make a base for the sculpture that is part of the sculpture itself. This fish is streamlined and simple. Feel free to make another type of fish after you try this one. This technique is adaptable to any type of fish.

MATERIALS AND TOOLS

Block of gray clay

**2 pieces of wood, 12 inches (30.5 cm) long,
$\frac{1}{8}$ inch (3 mm) thick★**

Cutting wire

Newspaper

Epsom salts and slip mixture (see page 17)

Paintbrushes

Serrated rib

Wooden paddles

Pin tool

Rubber kidney-shaped rib

**Wooden modeling tools in various shapes
and sizes**

Fettling knife

Small propane torch and striker★★

Safety glasses

Small wooden board

Turquoise and clear commercial glaze

★Wooden paint stirrers work well.

★★Please read safety procedures on page 65.

SHAPING THE BODY

1 To make a slab about $\frac{1}{8}$ inch (3 mm) thick I use the large wooden paint stirrers that paint stores give away. These stirrers are about $\frac{1}{8}$ inch (3 mm) thick; to make a thicker slab, just stack up more stirrers. Place the clay between the stirrers or slats of wood, spaced about 8 to 10 inches (20.3 to 25.4 cm) apart. Place the cutting wire on the stirrers, hold it flat, and pull the wire towards you until you cut a slab of clay free.

2 After cutting the slab this way, I like to "flip the slab out" to stretch the clay and make it thinner. Pick up the slab by one edge and throw it onto the table top. The idea is not to slam it down flat but rather to flip it out so that one end (the end opposite your hands) touches the table first, and then the force of the movement will stretch the clay out. Rotate your hands so you are picking up the slab from a different end each time you throw it down.

3 Flipping out the slab will give the edges a nice shape and thin out the clay.

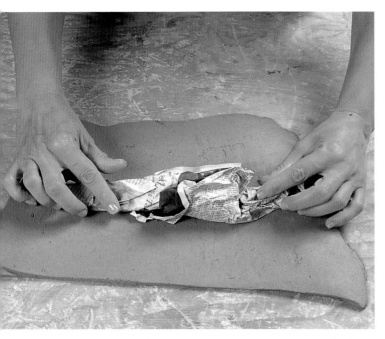

4 Crumple up some newspaper into a cylindrical shape and place it on the slab lengthwise.

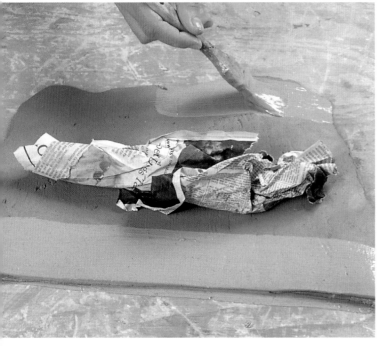

5 Brush slip on both ends of the slab.

6 Use the serrated rib to score the slab well.

7 Fold the slab over the newspaper.

8 Pinch the edges of the form closed. The newspaper inside will give it support.

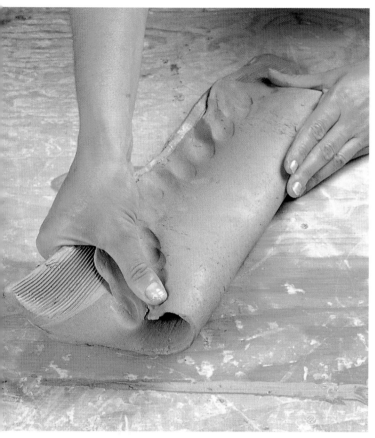

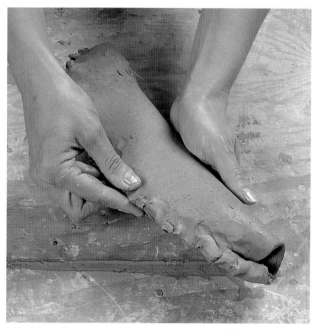

9 Pinch a little harder along the edge where the newspaper is: you are now starting to define the body of the fish.

11 Squeeze and join the seam together. It's important that there be sufficient slip between the two edges to make a secure joint.

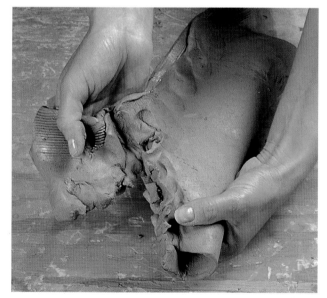

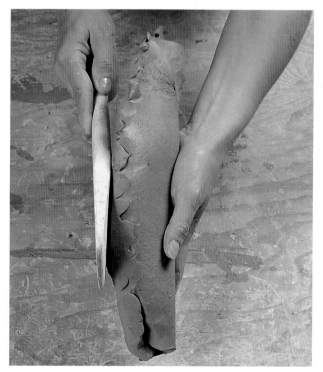

10 Pinch even harder, and tear off the clay along the pinchmarks. The form should be wider in the middle and taper at both ends. Different fish have different shape bodies; you can experiment later with different shapes once you learn this technique.

12 Gently paddle the seam closed. Remember to turn the paddle over or dry it off once it gets too wet, or it will begin to pull the clay apart instead of helping to join it. Be sure to make a few small pinholes in the body of the fish and in the head to release trapped air. This is very important, and failure to do so could lead to the piece exploding in the kiln.

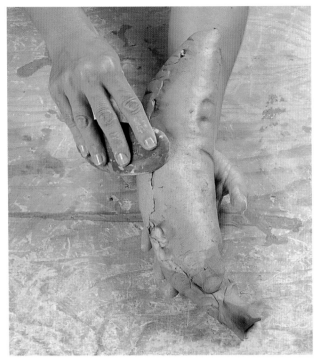

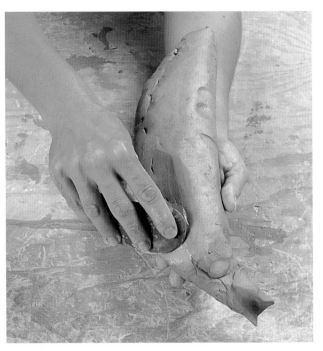

13 I like to use a rubber, kidney-shaped rib to smooth out the seam. You can use a little slip to lubricate the rib, but don't use too much or you'll weaken the seam. If the clay gets too soft, put it aside on something soft, such as a piece of foam or a rolled up cotton cloth. Let it stiffen up for awhile until it holds its shape better.

15 Use the rubber rib to blend these pieces into the form, sculpting as you work your way along the body.

MODELING THE FACE

1 At this point it might be a good idea to let the clay stiffen up a bit, if you haven't done so already. Then use a slant-edge modeling tool to draw the mouth of the fish.

14 If there are still some open parts in the seam or some places where the seam is very noticeable, brush on some slip and add small amounts of clay to fill in the gaps.

3 Turn the fish over, and using the pointed-end tool, push into the clay to create an eye cavity. I like to make the eye cavity deep and round.

2 Here's how to create fish lips: Hold the fish lengthwise in your hand. Work the modeling tools along the bottom section of the mouth; dig in a bit, then push the tool away from you. Turn the fish over and repeat this process on the other side. This is a good technique to use when you want to distinguish one part of a sculpture from another. By modeling or pushing the tool in one direction, away from another part or form, you give that area a distinct shape and set up a nice contrast between shapes, using direction and mass to help it look different. In this case, the lower part of the mouth is actually slightly deeper than the top, which creates the lips.

4 Right behind the eye, draw a semicircle; this will become a gill.

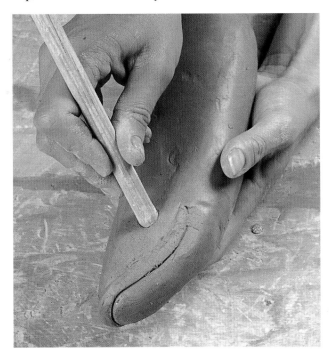

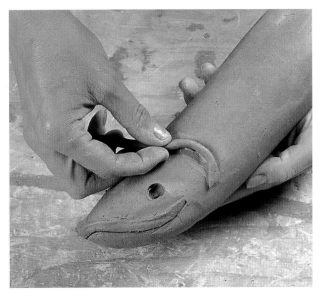

5 Roll out a small, thin coil. Slip and score the carved semicircle, and add the small coil.

6   Attach the coil using your wooden tool.

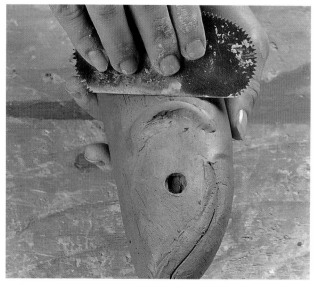

7   Smooth the area behind the gill with a rib tool.

8   Dab a little slip into the eye cavity. Roll out a small, round ball of clay and put it into the eye socket.

MAKING THE TAIL

1   Roll out two coils about 5 inches (12.7 cm) long. By rolling with more pressure on one end, you can taper the form to make it wider at one end and narrower at the other. This tapering technique is very important because it adds movement to the form once you add it on.

2   Flatten the forms a bit using the palm of your hand. Look closely at the clay—you might see the imprint of your skin on the clay, a rather nice texture.

3   Now "flip out" the flattened coils like we did the slab at the beginning of this project. It might take practice to get it right, but once you're able to do this you'll have learned a valuable technique.

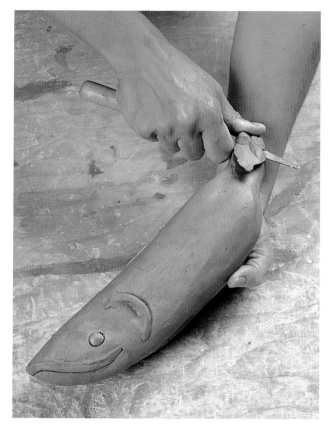

4 Use the fettling knife to trim down the sides of the fish where these flattened coils will join it to make the tail.

5 All right now, get ready for a great technique. I like to use a small propane torch to rapidly stiffen up the clay. These torches are available at hardware stores and are invaluable for clay sculpture work. They are also very dangerous if not used properly, so let's take a moment to review some safety procedures.

SAFETY PROCEDURES

A Purchase a striker when you purchase the torch, and use it to light the torch. Using matches or a lighter to light the torch is dangerous.

B Wear safety glasses.

C When lighting the torch, face it away from you. Turn on the gas slowly, opening the valve only a little until you hear the gas escape; then use the striker to light it.

D Turn off the torch when you're not going to use it right away.

E Don't use the torch around flammable materials.

F Keep a container of water or a spray bottle handy to put out flames.

G Read and understand all the instructions that come with the torch.

If you're not comfortable using the torch, simply set the flattened coils aside on a piece of newspaper, cover the fish with plastic, and wait until they are stiff enough to attach to the fish. When you can hold the coils, and they stand up and hold their shape, they're ready; this usually happens in 30 to 60 minutes.

If you do use the torch, lay the fish down on its side, slip and score the area where the flattened coil will be, and attach the coil. Light the torch. With the flame about 2 or 3 inches (5 to 7.6 cm) away from the clay, move it slowly back and forth over the clay for a one or two minutes in each area. Take the torch away, and you'll see steam coming off the clay as water evaporates. The clay will become stiffer now: it should hold its shape and not droop or bend.

6 Pick up the fish by the body so the tail is hanging free, and repeat the process; be careful not to dry out the clay too much.

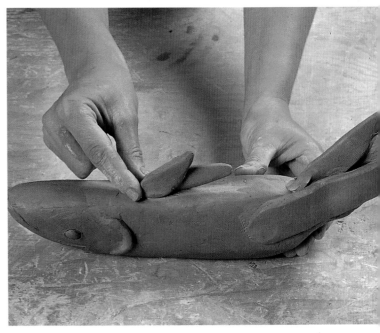

8 Attach two small, flattened coils on the top of the fish body to create fins. Set the piece aside to stiffen up while you start making a base for the sculpture.

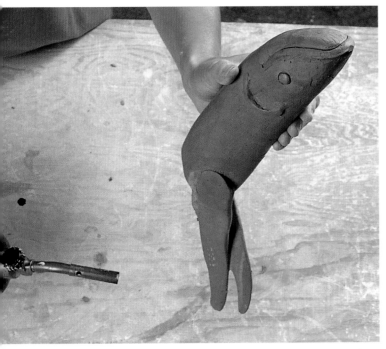

7 Add the other long tail piece to the other side and repeat the process. Add the smaller tall piece in between.

MAKING THE BASE

1 Make a small slab and cut from it an oval shape that is about the same length as the body of the fish (not including the head and tail). Flip the slab out onto the tabletop.

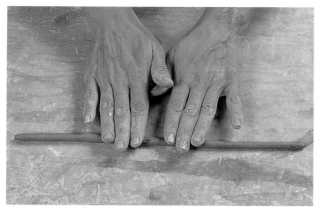

2 Roll out a ⅜-inch-thick (1 cm) coil long enough to encircle the outer edge of the oval slab. Roll from the middle of the coil outward using light, firm pressure.

3 Cover the wooden board with a piece of scrap paper and place the slab on top. Slip and score the base and attach the coil.

4 Use your modeling tool to press down the coil and join it to the base on the inside of the form.

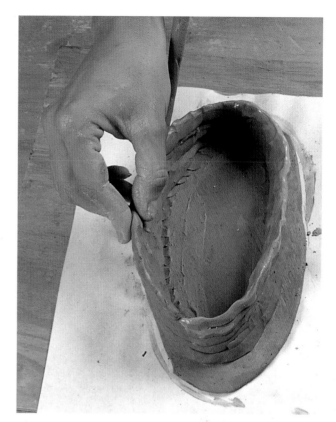

5 Continue adding coils until the form is 3 to 4 inches (7.6 to 10 cm) high. On the inside of the form only, use the tool to join each coil to the one under it and to blend the edges where they meet. Don't blend the coil edges on the front side of the base—you want to be able to see the round shape of the coil.

6 Roll out some small, thin coils, and taper them the way you tapered the tail coils. Then roll them into spiral shapes, with the thin tapered point as the beginning of the spiral.

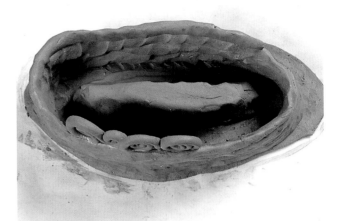

7 Slip, score, and attach these shapes to the inside of the form.

8 Make a thick coil and attach it to the bottom of the inside of the form. This coil should be very soft so that you can sit the fish on it and still be able to adjust the position of the fish.

9 Gently place the fish into the base to check how it fits. You can adjust the base to make it wider or narrower by pushing in lightly on the coils or pressing outward. Adjust its position; move the fish back and forth. Later on, after we paint it with underglaze, we'll attach the fish permanently.

Finishing the Fish

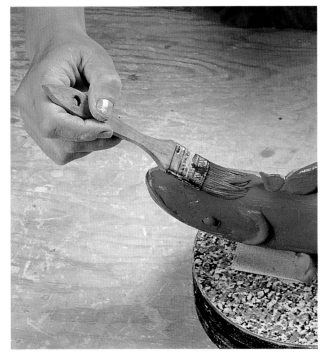

1 Because I like to have layers of color on some pieces, I often use slips on clay sculptures. This piece calls for a bright color, so I have chosen a blue-green commercial underglaze. Apply two layers with a soft paintbrush, being sure to cover all the areas of the fish. Since the base will be glazed turquoise, don't put any slip on it.

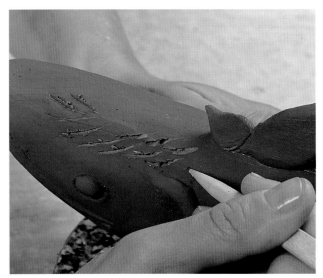

2 Let the underglaze dry awhile before continuing. Since we're using a light gray clay, we can use a technique called *sgrafitto*; use a modeling tool to scratch through the underglaze and reveal the clay color underneath. This technique is even more effective when you use a white clay body.

3 Texture the entire body of the fish to add richness and contrast to the surface. Apply plenty of thick slip on both the bottom of the fish and the center coil in the base; score the bottom of the fish and lower it onto its base, making sure it adheres well to the center coil.

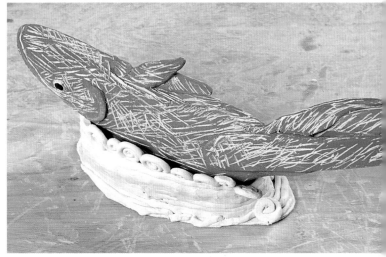

4 Bisque fire the fish and the base.

5 Apply the turquoise glaze to the base. Apply a clear glaze to the body of the fish to highlight the rich underglaze color. Follow the directions on the glaze container, which generally call for two to three coats of glaze.

6 Fire the piece to Δ6 in an electric kiln.

THE HEAD IN CLAY

This piece is particularly expressive, and an excellent way to learn more about figurative sculpture. It requires some patience; it's a good idea to practice sculpting the head a few times before trying the whole project. The focus of the sculpture is the features on the face, their texture and the angle at which the head meets the body.

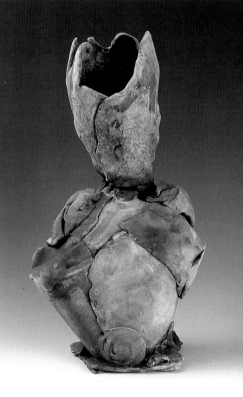

MATERIALS AND TOOLS

Clay

Epsom salts and slip mixture (see page 17)

Paintbrushes

Newspaper

Wooden paddles

Turntable

Wooden modeling tools in various sizes and shapes

White terra sigillata

Materials for smoke firing: sawdust, 3 to 4 bricks, newspaper, matches, metal trash container, heavy gloves★

★See step 4 on page 79 for details.

SHAPING THE TORSO-BASE

1 Roll and throw out three slabs about ⅜ inch (1 cm) thick, ranging in size from approximately 12 x 15 inches (31 to 38 cm) to 16 x 22 inches (41 to 56 cm). These will be used to shape the base, head, and torso.

2 Brush a generous amount of the Epsom salts and slip mixture around the edge of the largest slab.

3 Scrunch up some newspaper and place it in the center of the slab. This will provide support for the form.

4 Fold the slab over, making sure there is plenty of slip between the folded sections.

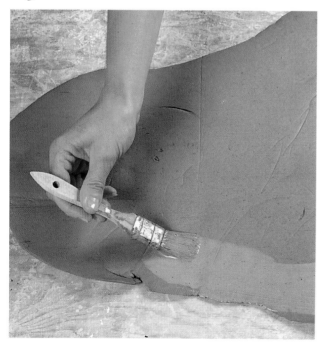

71

5 Push the newspaper down lightly into the bottom of the folded form. Add more newspaper for support.

7 Paddle in the sides and top to create folds and textures.

6 Paddle the sides and bottom to seal the form. Paddling also gives a nice surface to the clay. I try to keep my hands from making impressions or textures on the surface and let the paddle leave its distinct texture. Dry off the paddle or switch to a new one as it begins to get wet from the clay.

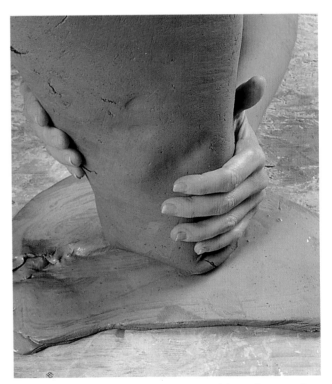

8 Brush slip onto the smallest slab and press the form onto it.

9 Fold this slab into the larger form, creating appealing folds and textures.

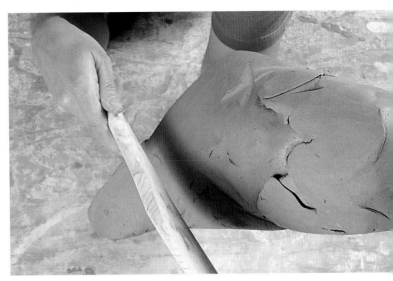

11 Place one hand inside the torso-base and continue to paddle it, especially the bottom, so it will sit level. Continue to paddle the form to create appealing folds and seams. Place the piece on a turntable and set it aside.

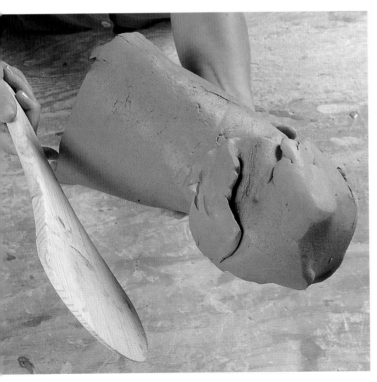

10 Hold the form and folded slab securely in one hand and turn it over. Paddle to attach the slab securely to the form. Notice how the clay moves and creases as you lightly paddle it.

SHAPING THE HEAD

1 Apply slip to the third slab, coating one inside and one outside edge; this piece will be the head. Fold the slab into a conical shape. You need to work quickly; the clay has to be soft enough to model with your fingers yet firm enough to hold its own weight.

2 The modeling of the head is tricky. I use the skinlike quality of the clay to give an impression of flesh and bone. The idea is to press in for hollows, such as the eyes, and press out for masses, such as the cheekbones. Place one hand inside the form and, with your fingers, push out for the nose. Then gently stroke the clay outward to form the shape. With the other hand press in for the eye cavities.

3 Place one hand inside the form and one outside. Place the outside hand in a horizontal position just below the inside hand and stroke outward with the hand that is inside the form to shape the top lip. As you do this, press in slightly with the outside hand to form a small horizontal cavity.

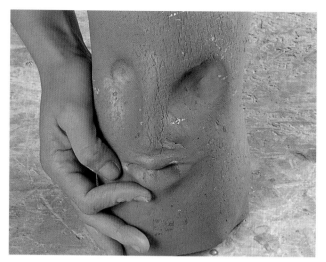

4 Drop the outside hand a bit and push out from the inside to model the bottom lip. The idea is to create a natural modeling by pushing in and out, as opposed to cutting into the clay, or adding on large pieces of clay and then smoothing them out. The features should emerge smoothly and naturally from the form.

5 Repeat this process to model the chin.

74

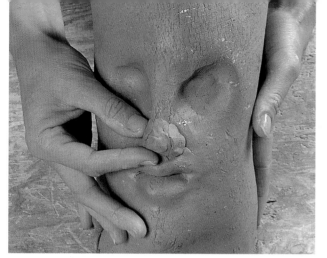

6 It may be necessary to add small bits of clay to the nose to build it up. Avoid a "flat" nose; the nose is a prominent feature of the face and extends off of it quite a bit.

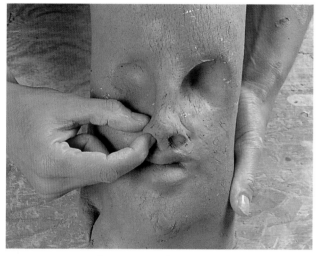

7 Use your fingers to add nostrils and cavities to the nose.

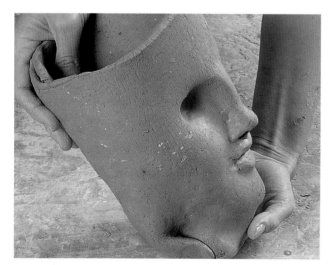

8 Here is a side view: notice how far off the face the nose extends and how deep the eye cavities are.

9 Use a pointed-end modeling tool to define the edge of the nostril.

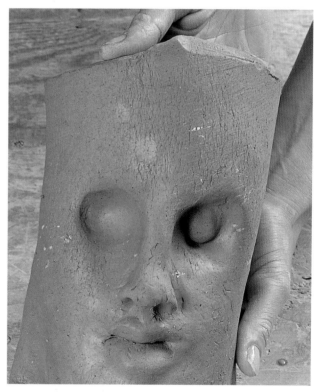

10 Place one hand inside the head and stroke the clay outward little by little to create the eye. This method gives the impression of a closed eyelid. Be careful not to tear the clay.

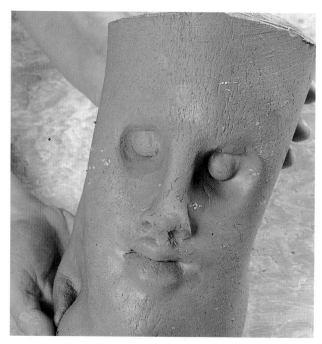

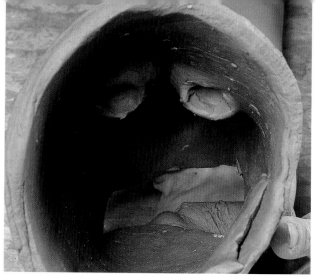

11 Here's a view of the head; notice how natural the textures are.

13 Looking inside the form you can see how the pushing out and pressing in has formed the features.

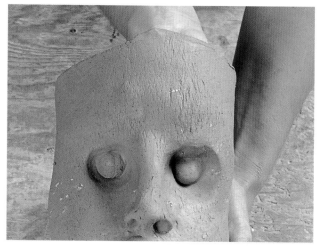

12 This view shows how the closed eyelid is far back from the level of the face plane. The way light plays across the highs and lows of the face of a sculpture is important. Keeping the eye area shaded adds softness and mystery to the face.

14 Run your hand along the inside to create a prominence along the brow and forehead.

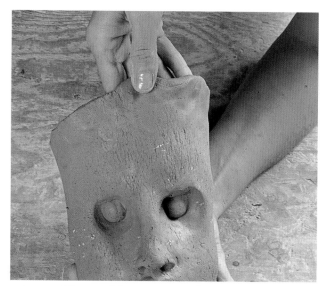

15 If you wish, you can pull lightly on the head to elongate it and open the features up a little. Set the head aside for awhile and let it stiffen up.

4 Gather up your piece, some sawdust and newspaper, matches, a few bricks, and a metal trash container. Notice the holes that have been drilled in the container to permit air to enter. Place the container on top of a few bricks. The container will get very hot, so be careful to leave lots of room around it and underneath it for air to circulate. Make sure the container is placed far away from any combustibles.

7 Set fire to the newspaper, and wait to make sure the sawdust is ignited well.

5 Place a layer of sawdust about 8 inches (20 cm) deep in the container and place the piece on top.

6 Cover up the work completely with sawdust, and place some crumpled newspaper on top.

8 Cover the container, with the lid slightly ajar to let in air. When you're sure the sawdust is burning well, cover the container tightly with the lid. Check periodically to make sure it's still burning. When a smoke firing is done properly, small wisps of smoke should escape from the lid throughout the firing. When all the sawdust has burned away and the container is cool, remove your work; you may need gloves. Clean the head and bust with water and a little soap to get rid of unburned sawdust and carbon deposits.

STANDING FIGURE

In this project we will create a stylized human form that demonstrates how clay can be used to quickly create a standing figure. The proportions are important here; the relationships between legs and torso are exaggerated to give the figure a feeling of isolation. These techniques can be adapted to larger figures or sculptures. A key technique here is to wrap newspaper around a cylinder to help you create an armature around which to wrap a clay slab. The clay is then raised up to a standing position and the cylinder removed. The newspaper acts as a separator that allows you to remove the cylinder without disturbing the clay.

MATERIALS AND TOOLS

Clay

Newspaper

2 wooden dowel rods, 1 inch (2.5 cm) thick

1 wooden dowel, ½ inch (1.3 cm) thick

Epsom salts and slip mixture (see page 17)

Paintbrushes

Fettling knife

★Propane torch and striker

Wooden paddle

Wooden modeling tools in various shapes and sizes

Matte copper glaze

★Please read the safety procedures on page 65.

SHAPING THE BODY

1 Roll out three or four slabs about ¼ inch (6 mm) thick; two will be for the legs, and the rest for the body and head. The slabs here measure about 8 inches (20 cm) long and 5 inches (12.7 cm) wide. (Details about cutting and rolling out slabs appear on page 59.)

2 To create the armature for the legs, wrap a 1-inch (2.5 cm) dowel in newspaper. You can use a thinner dowel, depending on how thick you want the legs to be. To form the other leg, repeat this process with the other 1-inch-thick (2.5 cm) dowel and another slab.

3 Apply slip to the edges of the slab. Fold the clay tightly around the dowel.

4 Push the two ends of the clay together to seal the tube shape. To avoid a thick overlap at the joint, cut away the excess clay by holding the fettling knife at a 45° angle. Repeat this process for the other leg form.

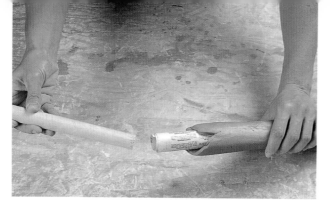

5 Set the form aside to stiffen, then reach in and pull out the dowel. Don't let the dowel sit in the form too long or the clay will shrink around it and trap it. Although drying times will depend on room temperature, the form should stiffen up in about 20 minutes.

6 To form the base, roll out a small, round slab about ⅜ inch (1 cm) thick and 6 to 8 inches (15 to 20 cm) in diameter. Apply slip to the bottom of the two leg forms and one side of the base, score the base well, and attach the legs.

7 Apply slip to the upper part of the two leg forms, and press them together.

8 Tear some small pieces of clay from one of the remaining slabs. Apply slip to the tops of the leg forms, and attach these small pieces to form the torso. Look for a loose, folding texture to develop from this technique. Remember to use plenty of slip and to squeeze the pieces together with your fingers.

9 Place more pieces on the form to build up shape and create texture.

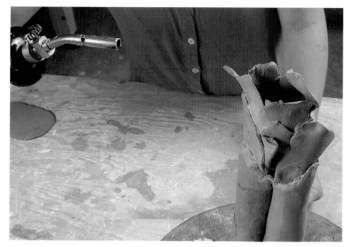

10 You are now ready to use the torch to accelerate the stiffening up of the torso. Holding the propane torch about 16 inches (40 cm) away from the form, slowly pass the flame over the clay for two or three minutes. Don't hold the flame in one spot for too long or the clay will crack and pieces will pop off. If you don't want to dry the clay in this manner, simply set the form aside on a piece of newspaper, cover it with plastic, and wait until it is stiff.

11 Now that the torso is stiff, use the wooden paddle to shape it.

SHAPING THE HEAD

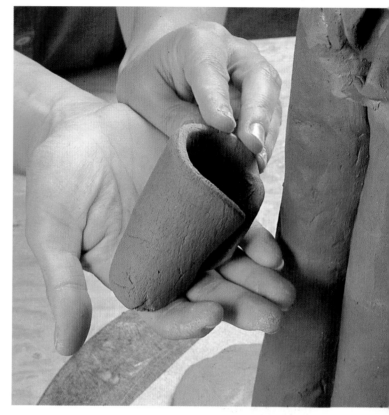

1 Use a small slab about ¼ inch (6 mm) thick for the head, and shape it into a cone shape. Keep in mind the proportion of the head to the body.

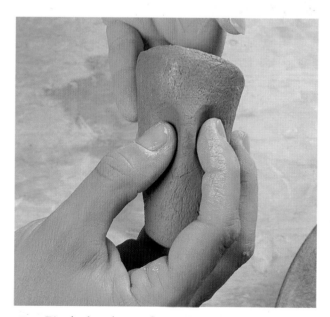

2 Pinch the clay to form two eye cavities.

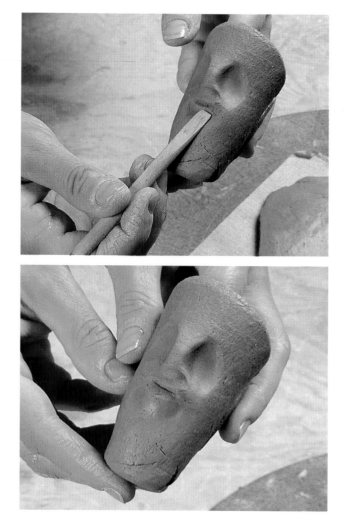

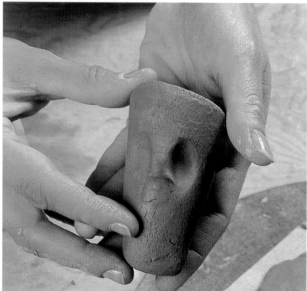

3 Hold your finger across the clay and push in to shape the nose.

4 Use a flat-end modeling tool to create the mouth.

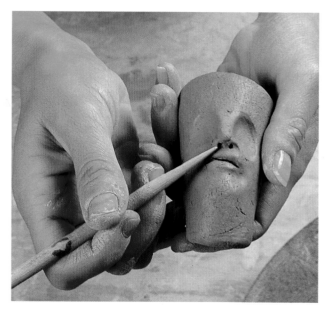

5 Use a pointed-end tool to make the nostrils.

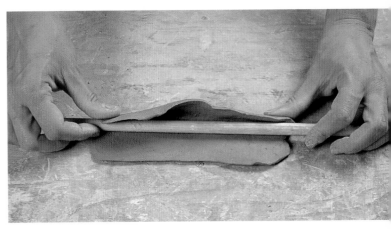

8 Roll out two thin slabs about 4 to 5 inches (10 to 12.7 cm) in length and ⅛ inch (3 mm) thick: these will be the arms. Slump the clay over the ½-inch-thick (1.3 cm) dowel rod. You can use newspaper if you want, but generally you don't need to when the slab cylinders are this small. Be sure to use slip to join the slab edges the way you did before.

6 Reach into the head form with your flat-end tool and gently stroke outward behind the eye cavity to push out the clay; this will give the appearance of a closed eyelid. Be careful not to push out too hard or you will rip the clay; if you push out too much, the face will have a "bug-eyed" appearance. If these things happen, don't worry; just paint a little slip on the area and push the clay back, or add a little clay and re-sculpt the area.

9 Paint slip on the torso and attach one of the arms to the body. I like to leave a lot of the folds and natural textures of the clay showing.

7 Paint some slip on the top of the torso, score the area, and attach the head to the torso. Position the head in a way that pleases you.

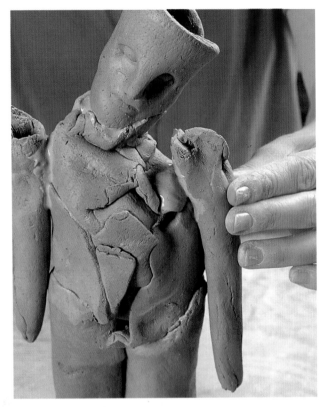

10 Attach the other arm in the same manner. I like to put one arm slightly below the other for contrast and to allow the figure to convey feeling.

FINISHING THE FIGURE

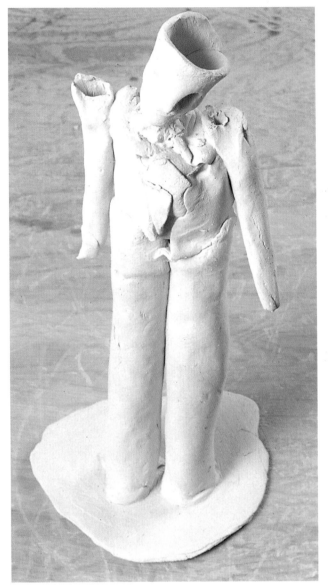

1 Here's how the figure looks after it has been bisque fired.

2 Bisque fire the figure. (Note: Because I planned to raku-fire the figure, I bisque fired it to Δ04, a little higher than usual, to give it added strength. Then I sprayed a thin layer of dry, matte copper glaze on it to give the piece a little color without covering over the textures and folds in the clay. I left a good deal of the body unglazed and naturally dark from the smoke.

WALL SCULPTURE

Of all the projects in this book, only this wall sculpture can be considered pure abstract or nonrepresentational art. It relies on the relationship between parts to achieve grace and beauty. Sometimes leaving out recognizable elements, such as birds or flowers, can be liberating. By using texture, color, and spatial relationships, we can invoke the same kind of feelings and responses that representational objects do, but in a more mysterious and deep manner. The viewer must search for things in the sculpture, instead of being presented with them right away.

Feel free to alter the dimensions or number of components in this piece. Make a few sculptures like this and slowly work up to more complex arrangements.

MATERIALS AND TOOLS

Red earthenware clay

Serrated rib

Red slip mixed with Epsom salts
(see page 17)

Paintbrushes

Small wooden board

Sheet of white paper

Fettling knife

Wooden modeling tools in various
sizes and shapes

Ruler

White slip

Artist's paintbrush

Natural sponge

Several small stones, twigs, and/or pods

Silicone glue

Epoxy glue

Supplies for hanging wall piece
(see step 3, page 92)

BUILDING THE BOX

1 Roll out two slabs, each about 8 x 12 inches (20 x 30.5 cm), and ⅛ inch (3 mm) thick.

Since this will be a wall piece, we don't want it to be too heavy. Place the slabs on the wooden board covered with a piece of white paper; the white paper will help you focus on the composition and make it easier to remove the piece from the board for firing. Cut or tear out a smaller strip, slip and score the back of it with red slip, and attach it to the larger slab. When placing pieces together for a wall piece, think about placement and the relationship between the parts. Put down the clay pieces in areas and in relationships that appeal to you. Run your finger lightly along the bottom surface of the wall piece, about 2 inches (5 cm) up from the bottom. Fold up the clay along that line.

2 Use the fettling knife to cut out three small rectangles, about 1 x 2 inches (2.5 x 5 cm). Their purpose is to visually separate the folded up slab from the one we are about to make and attach. Subtle techniques like this lend visual interest to your work. Cut or tear a long rectangular shape from your scrap slab of clay.

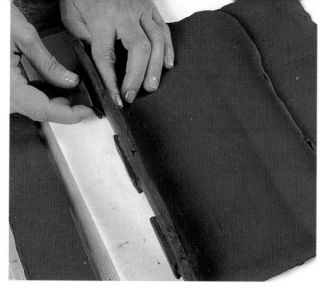

3 Slip and score the small rectangles, and attach them to the underside of the folded up form.

4 Slip and score the long rectangle, and attach it to the small rectangles, which now act as spacers and create a nice, linear shadow at the bottom of the piece.

5 Cut or tear two smaller rectangular shapes, and attach them along the sides of the form to create a shallow boxlike form. This will give us a separate area within the wall piece where we can compose with clay forms.

6 Use the flat-end modeling tool to smooth the seams and take away any scoring marks from the side pieces.

ADDING THE SHAPES

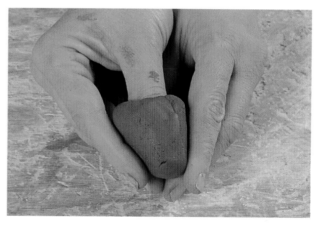

1 Now we will make the shapes to place on the wall piece. Make a small pinch pot.

2 Using the edge of a ruler or a small board, texture the pot.

3 Roll out a coil about the thickness of your finger. Use a straight-edge modeling tool to roll it and texture it.

4 Use a ruler or a board to slightly flatten the coil.

5 Here are some of the possibilities for shapes made with these techniques. Experiment with making your own different shapes.

6 Place the shapes in the "box," but don't attach them yet. Notice how it helps that they are isolated in the wall piece; attention is focused on them and gives us a specific place to look, a "center" to the work. Move the parts around and compose with them until you arrive at an arrangement you like.

7 Brush a little white slip on one of the pieces; this will provide a nice contrast to the dark clay when it's fired.

8 After the slip has dried a bit, wipe it off with a damp sponge, leaving white slip only in the recesses.

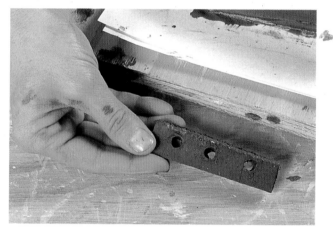

9 Cut a narrow rectangle and put a few holes in it. We will use this to raise up one of the pieces higher than the others. This is a way to create even more interest by changing the level at which the clay shapes sit in relation to each other.

10 Score and slip one long edge of the rectangle, and attach it to the wall piece, smoothing the seams with a modeling tool.

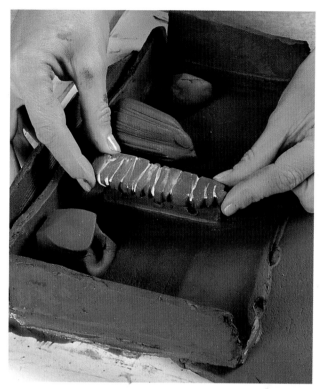

11 Score and slip the back of the flattened coil piece, and attach it to the rectangular spacer, with the white slip side facing up.

12 Make three small clay balls. Slip, score, and attach them to the wall piece where the largest of the clay shapes will be attached. These will also act to raise up the form, so it's at a different level from the rest.

13 Slip and score the larger piece, and set it on the three balls so that the balls are covered and not visible. This will help give the impression that the piece is floating off the back surface. Now that you have two pieces attached, you may want to adjust the position of the other two pieces.

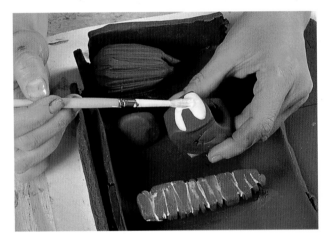

14 Paint white slip on the next largest piece on part of the front; this will draw attention to it and help balance the composition visually.

15 Slip, score, and attach the piece, painted side up, to the wall piece.

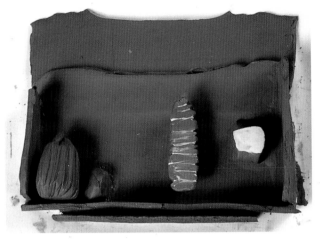

16 Slip, score, and attach the final shape to the wall piece. Cover it with plastic and let it dry slowly.

FINISHING THE PIECE

1 Fire the piece to Δ2 in an electric kiln, a somewhat higher than usual temperature for earthenware. Firing it higher brings out the rich, red color of the clay.

2 Take a walk outdoors to collect stones, twigs, and other natural elements that will complement the composition. Since the red clay color is already established, look for shapes and colors to go with it. You can attach these other elements using silicone glue. I like this thick and sticky glue; it takes awhile to dry which gives you time to move the additions around, and it also fills in gaps.

3 To mount the wall piece, I usually cut a piece of plywood about ½ inch (1.3 cm) smaller than the clay sculpture, and then glue it to the back of the piece, using epoxy glue. This is a two-part glue that is available in any hardware store. I mix up a larger amount at once, and apply it to the wood. Then I place the sculpture face up on the wood, and adjust it so it's evenly spaced on the wood; then I let it set overnight. I place two small screws and some picture wire on the back to hang it. There are other ways to hang ceramic sculptures like this. If they are small—10 to 12 inches (25.4 to 30.5 cm)—you can use plate hangers. There are preshaped wire and spring clips used for displaying decorative plates. With a little adapting, they work fine and require no glue or screws. Some artists leave a little clay, in which they later make a hole, in the back of the sculpture as they shape it. After the piece is fired, they wind the picture wire through it.

CHAPTER FIVE

GALLERY

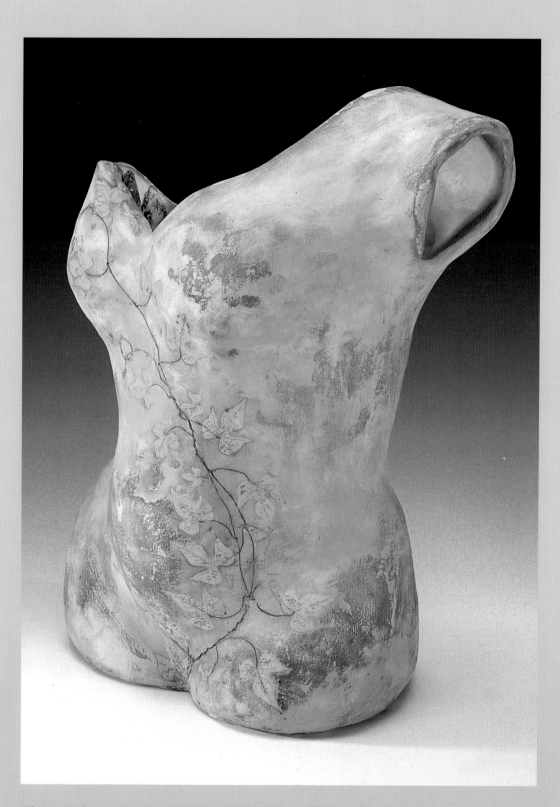

Chrysta Sylvester, *Earth Angel*, 1998. 24 x 38 x 40 in. (5.1 x 96.5 x 101.6 cm). Stoneware; coil built; natural vine inlay; chrome oxide terra sigillata, titanium oxide wash; low fired, Δ06; high fired, Δ6.
Photo by Melva Calder

94

Top left, page 94: **Bryan Hiveley**, *Blue Wave*, 1998. 54 x 28 x 17 in. (135 x 70 x 42.5 cm). Earthenware; slab and coil built; oxidation fired, Δ03. Photo by artist

Top right, page 94: **Megan Wolfe**, *Blood Yellow*, 1992. 29 x 29 x 5 in. (73.7 x 73.7 x 12.7 cm). Terra cotta; press molded, carved, pinch pots; bisque fired, Δ04; glaze fired, Δ08 to Δ04. Photo by artist

Bottom, page 94: **Vincent Burke**, *Gobstopper 3*, 1999. 18 x 24 x 10 in. (45 x 60 x 25 cm). Low-fire white earthenware; slab and slump molded construction; fired in electric kiln, Δ04. Photo by Vincent Burke

Above: **Deborah J. Weinstein**, *Fred*, 1999. 4 x 6 x 2 in. (10 x 15 x 5 cm). Δ5 porcelain; pinched over newspaper form, coils added; textured; underglazes, oxidation fired in electric kiln, Δ5.

Right: **Elyse Saperstein**, *Head Over Heels*, 1998. 22 x 12½ x 8 in. (55.9 x 31.8 x 20.3 cm). Earthenware; slab carved with bas-relief, some coils; glaze, wash fired in electric kiln, Δ05 to Δ06. Photo by John Cartano

Left, page 96: **Judy Geerts**, *Eggs in a Box*, 1997. 51 x 21 x 5 in. (127.5 x 52.5 x 12.5 cm). Smooth-bodied white raku clay; weighed equally while wet, pinched into forms; bisque fired, Δ04; black underglaze (interior) and copper matte glaze (exterior) raku fired with newspaper and sawdust reduction, Δ07; assembled in box. Photo by Larry Dikeman

Top right, page 96: **Vern Langhofer**, *Untitled*, 1999. 19 x 16 x 11 in. (47.5 x 24 x 27.5 cm). Raku; slab technique; fired in gas kiln, Δ06, ending with shredded paper and sawdust reduction. Photo by Mad Dog Studio

Bottom right, page 96: **David J. Babb**, *Locomotion*, 1997–98. 12 x 18 in. (30.5 x 45.7 cm). Stoneware; handbuilt; vinyl letters, glaze, high fired.

Above: **Mary Carolyn Obodzinski**, *Relic*, 1999. 8 x 17 x 5 in. (20.3 x 43.2 x 12.7 cm). Stoneware; slab built; textured with stamps; raku fired; gold leaf added to interior. Photo by Ann Nevills Photography

Right: **Marla Bollack**, *Triple-lobed Vessel with Weeping Buddha*, 1999. 7¼ x 7½ x 6 in. (18 x 18.8 x 15 cm). Red earthenware; pinched lobes, wheel-thrown, handbuilt; fired in electric kiln, Δ06. Photo by Tim Barnwell

Top: **Jane A. Archambeau**, *Hope Springs Eternal*, 1999. 22 x 18 x 12 in. (56 x 45.8 x 30.5 cm). White earthenware; press molded, slab built; brown lichen glaze, underglaze, found objects multifired in electric kiln, Δ04 to Δ06. Photo by Corey Gray

Left: **David Hiltner**, *White Salmon U-boat*, 1999. 10½ x 13½x 6 in. (26.7 x 34.3 x 15.2 cm). Stoneware; slabs rolled, textured with rope; form handbuilt; salmon heads press molded and sprigged onto sides of form; white slip salt fired, Δ10.

Photo by Linda Robinson

Top left: **Juan Granados**, *Seed & Sprout*, 1999. 27 x 15 x 10 in. (68.6 x 38.1 x 25.4 cm). Earthenware; slab formed, handbuilt, pinched-formed additions; bisque oxidation fired in gas kiln, Δ04; glaze oxidation fired in electric kiln, Δ06. Photo by Jon Q. Thompson

Top right: **Carol Townsend**, *Chairs in Mind*, 1999. Low-fire clay; slab built; slips, sgraffito patterning; reduction fired, Δ6. Photo by K.C. Kratt

Right: **Ken Eastman**, *Untitled Vessel*, 1999. 8 x 18 x 11 in. (21 x 46 x 28 cm.). White stoneware with grog; slab built; oxides, colored slips, oxidation fired in electric kiln, 3304 °F (1180°C). Photo by artist

Top left: **LuAnne Tackett Simpson**, *Silent Witness*, 1999. 20 x 12 x 8 in. (50.8 x 30.5 x 20.3 cm). Stoneware with grog; press-molded slabs, coils, untextured slabs; velvet underglazes, diluted glaze; bisque fired, Δ02; multi-fired with velvets, oxides, glazes. Photo by artist

Top right: **Marie E.v.B. Gibbons**, *Lady of the House*, 1999. 20 x 12 x 10 in. (50 x 30 x 25 cm). Low-fire white clay, wooden base, bone drawer pulls; handbuilt, carved, scratched; fired in electric kiln, Δ04; cold finishes of acrylics, prisma color, pencil, India ink. Photo by John Bonath (Mad Dog Studio)

Left: **Megan Dull**, *Listening to the Holy in My Own Soul*, 1998. 22 x 14 x 18 in. (55.8 x 35.5 x 45.8 cm). White stoneware; torso coil built, textured; portal, fish slab built; figure solid, carved then hollowed out; red terra sigillata sprayed on greenware; black copper oxide washes over bisque; fired in gas kiln, Δ1. Photo by artist

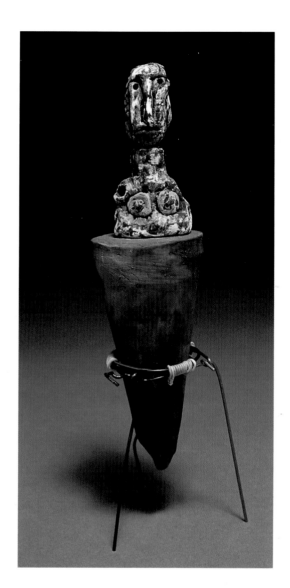

Top left: **Frank Shelton**, *Untitled*, 1999. 14 x 5 x
4½ in. (35.5 x 12.8 x 11.5 cm). Red earthenware;
handbuilt; multi-fired with oxides, underglazes in
electric kiln, Δ04, Δ05. Photo by Bart Kasten

Top right: **Megan Dull**, *Sister Image: The Revealing
of All We Never Knew About Her*, 1996. 19½ x 14 x
9 in. (49.5 x 35.5 x 22.8 cm). White stoneware; coil
built; surface pressed with clay stamps, burnished;
terra sigillata with crocus martis oxide fired in electric kiln, Δ04; black copper oxide wash, Δ04.
Photo by artist

Right: **Judith Nicolaidis**, *Crucible*, 1999. 26 x 17 x
11½ in. (66 x 43 x 29.3 cm). White raku clay; slab
and coil built; small elements modelled, carved, cut,
hollowed, reassembled, pinched; underglazes, bisque
fired in electric kiln, Δ04; glazes, underglazes fired in
electric kiln, Δ06; enamel paints for details.
Photo by artist

Left, page 102: **Robert L. Wood**, *Phoenix*, 1997. 8 x 5 x 5 ft. (2.5 x 1.5 x 1.5 m). Earthenware; slab construction; embedded with cone packs, pottery shards, kiln elements, glass; iron oxide, frit coloration fired in gas kiln, Δ3, light reduction. Photo by artist

Right, page 102: **J. Paul Sires**, *Wave House Vessel*, 9 x 2.5 x 2 ft. (2.7 x 0.8 x 0.6 m). Terra cotta; slab built, coil built; fired in gas kiln, Δ3. Photo by Center of the Earth Gallery

Above: **Kathy Triplett**, *The Garden After Sundown*, 1999. 3 x 40 ft. x 4 in. (0.9 x 12 m x 10.2 cm). Handbuilt tiles; terra sigillata, stains, glazes fired, Δ03. Photo by artist

Right: **Agustin de Andino**, *La Elefanta de Castilla*, 1998. 28½ x 14½ inches (73 x 37 cm). Made from Δ6 stoneware; slab and coil built; sgrafitto and carving in leather-hard state; bisque fired to Δ04; ceramic pigments, oxides, and glazes; oxidation fired in electric kiln, Δ5/6. Photos by Eric Borcherding

103

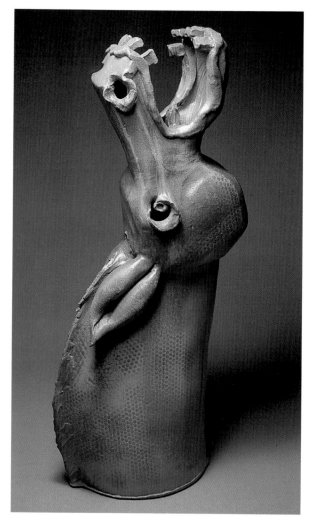

Top left: **Renée Azenaro**, *On the Edge*, 1989. 20 x 20 x 10 inches (51 x 51 x 25 cm). White stoneware; slab built; glaze, stains, oxides; oxidation fired, Δ5. Photo by artist

Top right: **Julie B. Hawthorne**, *Hold Tight Pony*, 1999. 32 x 14 x 9 in. (80 x 35 x 22.5 cm). Commercial brown clay; wheel–thrown, handrolled, handbuilt; clear glaze fired, Δ6. Photo by Chris Hawthorne

Left: **Norman D. Holen**, *Guinea Hen*, 1972. 10¾ x 13⅛ x 6½ in. (27.3 x 33.3 x 16.5 cm). Earthenware; press molded; fired in electric kiln, Δ05. Photo by Peter Lee

Top: **Pamela Timmons**, *Frogs*, 1999. 7 x 5 x 8 in. (17.8 x 12.5 x 20.3 cm) and 9 x 7 x 10 in. (22.8 x 17.8 x 25.5 cm). Stoneware; sculpted, hollowed; decorated with slip in grooves, sprayed glazes; oxidation fired, Δ6. Photo by Jim Wolnosky

Bottom left: **Sheila Orifice-Rogers**, *Madam of the Mill Pond*, 1998. 15 x 4½ in. (38.1 x 11.4 cm). Sculpture clay, red stoneware; wheel-thrown, slab built, pinched, carved, coil additions; bisque fired in electric kiln, Δ04; wood ash glaze with copper fired in electric kiln, Δ6. Photo by Steve Whitney

Bottom right: **Marilyn Richeda**, *Untitled*, 1999. 17 x 6 x ½ in. (43.3 x 15.3 x 1.3 cm). Red earthenware with medium grog; hand-stretched slab, cut-out animal abstract; textured glazes (grog, vermiculite, egg shells), glazes, underglazes, mason stains oxidation fired, Δ05. Photo by Smith-Baer

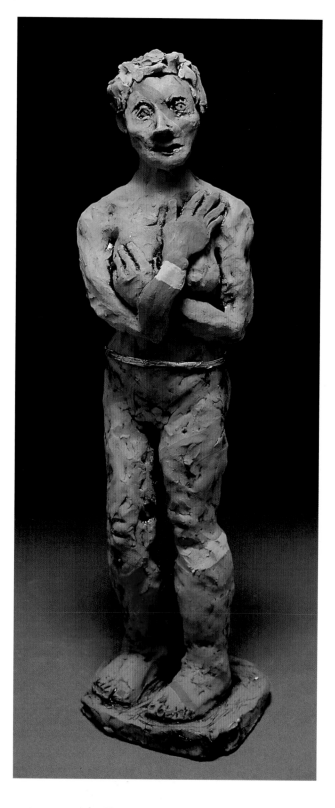

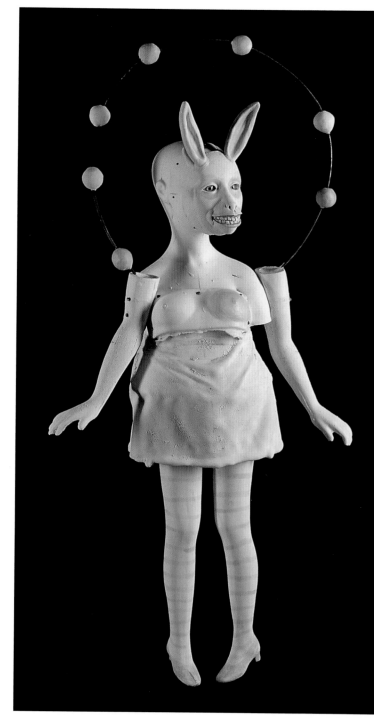

Left: **Wendy James**, *Untitled*, 1999. 27 x 8 x 4 in. (68.5 x 20.3 x 10 cm). Red clay with grog; pinched over dowels; bisque fired, Δ04; velvet underglazes fired, Δ05. Photo by Michael Noa

Above: **Lisa Clague**, *Trick*, 1999. 22 x 8 x 5 in. (55.8 x 20.3 x 12.8 cm). Low-fire white clay, low-fire white slip; head, torso slip cast; figure handbuilt; fabric dipped in slip and wrapped around figure; acrylic eyes glued behind mask; stains, glazes fired twice in electric kiln, Δ05, beeswax finish on mask and breast. Photo by Scott McCue

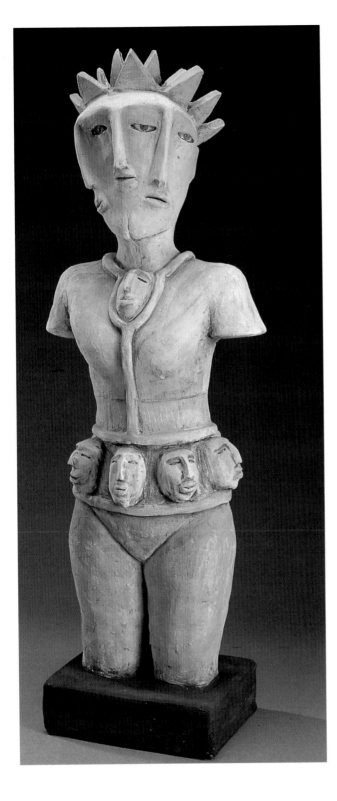

Above: **Barb Doll**, *Trinity*, 1998. 41 x 11 x 9 in. (104.1 x 27.9 x 22.9 cm). Stoneware; slab and coil built, pinched; fired, Δ4; finished with underglazes and slips. Photo by Bart Kastin

Right: **Melisa Cadell Comeau**, *She is Her Own*, 1998. 60 x 17 x 11 in. (152.4 x 43.2 x 27.9 cm). Red earthenware; coil and slab built, flanges added; oxidation fired in electric kiln, Δ04. Photo by Tom Mills

Top, page 108: **Christine Federighi**, *Structure,* 1998. 8 x 4 x 5 ft. (2.4 x 1.2 x 1.5 m). Stoneware, mixed media clay, metal parts; coil built, carved; oil patina, sealed; oxidation fired, Δ04. Photo by Fareed Al Mashat

Bottom, page 108: **Mitchell Messina**, *Wrench*, 1998. 3 x 3½ x 2½ ft. (0.9 x 1 x 0.7 m). White earthenware; coil and slab built, press molded; oxidation fired in electric kiln, Δ1; assembled, painted, stained. Photo by Walter Colley

Above: **Nan Smith**, *Visionary*, 1995. 9 x 25 x 35 ft. (2.8 x 7.6 x 10.7 m). Buff earthenware sculpture clay; molds, latex molds (of fabric) press molded with slabs, assembled; detailed, modelled; bisque fired in electric kiln, Δ06; airbrushed under-glazes, glazes fired in electric kiln, Δ03. Photo by Allen Cheuvront

Top left: **Dave Kellum**, *Juvenile Crime Stories*, 1999. 17 x 13 x 10 in. (43.2 x 33 x 25.4 cm). White raku clay with kyanite; slab built; underglazes, clear matte glaze applied to greenware; oxidation fired in electric kiln, Δ04. Photo by artist

Top right: **Claire Salzberg**, *Shiller's Fabric Store*, 1992. 16 x 12 in. (40 x 30 cm). Photo by Claire Salzberg

Left: **John E. Tobin, Jr.**, *Net Jam*, 1999. 9 x 11 x 9½ in. (22.8 x 28 x 24 cm). Stoneware; slab built, oriental coiling; added to notebook computer; acrylic paints, magazine collage; fired in electric kiln, Δ4. Photo by artist

110

Top: **Laura Wilensky**,
Something Sweet (hydrangea teapot), 1998. 4½ x 8¼ x 7 in.
(11.5 x 20.5 x 17.5 cm).
Porcelain; slab and coil built;
handpainted underglaze stains,
china paints; fired in electric
kiln, Δ10, Δ018. Photo by Storm
Photo

Right: **Dana Goodman**, *The Pig that Couldn't be Eaten All at One Time*, 1997. 42 x 36 x 20 in. (106.7 x 91.4 x 50.8 cm).
Earthenware; altered, press
molded slabs, carved surfaces;
fired in gas kiln, Δ04. Photo by
Oxford Gallery, Rochester, New York

Above: **David Traylor**, *marker.bowl.15*, 1999. 6 x 15 x 15 in. (15 x 37.5 x 37.5 cm). Δ6 stoneware with grog; press molded, coil built, slab made and torn for attachments, modified extruded coils. Photo by Doug Yaple

Left: **Marla Bollack**, *Double-lobed Vessel with Lizard*, 1999. 6½ x 7¼ x 5½ in. (16.3 x 18 x 13.8 cm). Red earthenware; pinched balls, rolled coils, handbuilt; fired in electric kiln, Δ06. Photo by Tim Barnwell

Top left, page 113: **Ann Marie Perry**, *Grind*, 1998. 24 x 22 x 15 in. (61 x 55.8 x 38 cm). Low-fire white clay; wheel-thrown, slab built, press molded; textured slips bisque fired, Δ04; over-glazes, oxides, metallic glazes fired, Δ04. Photo by Ann Perry

Top right, page 113: **David Traylor**, *marker.stone.8*, 1999. 13 x 14 x 11 in. (32.5 x 35 x 27.5 cm). Δ6 stoneware; body coil built; attachments handbuilt, extruded; oxidation in electric kiln, Δ6. Photo by Doug Yaple

Bottom, page 113: **Linda Hansen Mau,** *Tea for Two*, 1998. 7 x 11 x 6 in. and 3 x 5 x 3 in. (17.8 x 27.9 x 15.2 and 7.6 x 12.7 x 7.6 cm). Porcelain paper clay; slips applied to fabricated teapot (galvanized steel hardware cloth); red terra sigillata; bisque fired, Δ04; smoked in open wash tub with newspaper. Photo by Lynn Hunton

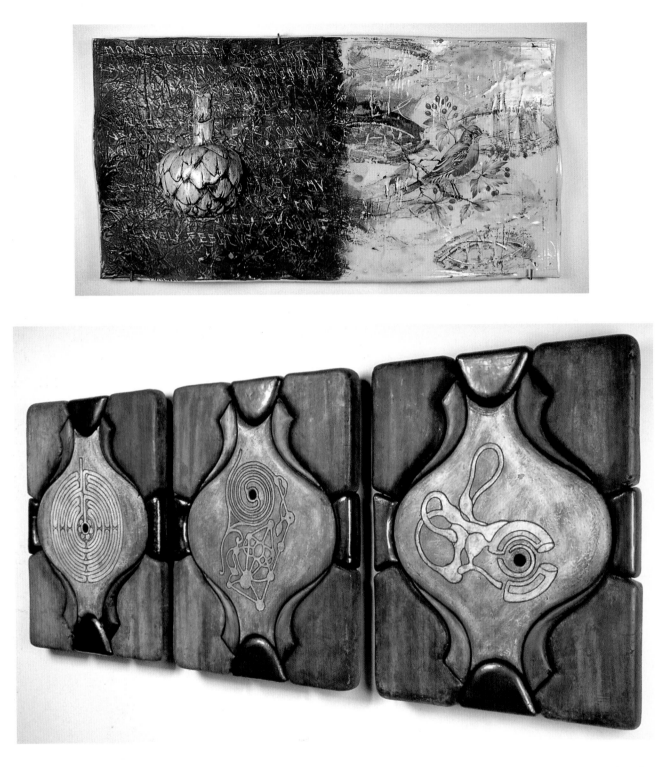

Top: **Pamela Pemberton**, *Linger and Listen*, 1999. 15 x 25 x ¼ in. (38 x 63.5 x 0.5 cm). Low-fire paper clay; clay monoprint; images drawn into plaster slab with layer of colored slip, covered with numerous layers of casting slip; bisque and glaze fired, Δ04; decal fired, Δ020; three-dimensional objects added. Photo by artist

Bottom: **Cary Esser**, *Labyrinth: Chartres, Maze, Ear Canal* (series of three bas-relief panels), 1999. 29 x 22 x 3 in. (73.7 x 55.9 x 7.6 cm) each. Red earthenware; tile sections mounted on wooden panels, press molded, incised; terra sigillata, low-fire glaze oxidation fired, Δ04. Photo by Jeff Bruce

Top left: **Leah Hardy**, *Subconscious Soliloquy*, 1999. 13 x 10½ x 4 in. (32.5 x 26.3 x 10 cm). Earthenware; slab-built, hand-modelled; low-fire glaze, terra sigillata, and oxides fired in electric kiln, Δ04. Photo by artist

Top right: **Diane Eisenbach**, *Lichen*, 1997. 12 x 12 x 2 in. (30 x 30 x 5 cm). Stoneware, porcelain; slab built from clay and organic materials; stains and glazes oxidation fired, Δ5; hand-made drawing on paper added to piece after firing. Photo by artist

Bottom left: **Steven C. Hewitt**, *Take-Out Box*, 1998. 15 x 15 x 2 in. (38 x 38 x 5 cm). Porcelain; slab on wood; underglaze, overglaze crackle; fired in electric kiln, Δ6. Photo by artist

Bottom right: **William B. Hogan**, *Peter's Fish Story*, 1996. 28 x 19½ x 2 in. (71 x 49.5 x 5 cm). Terra cotta; bas-relief; fired, Δ05. Photo by artist

115

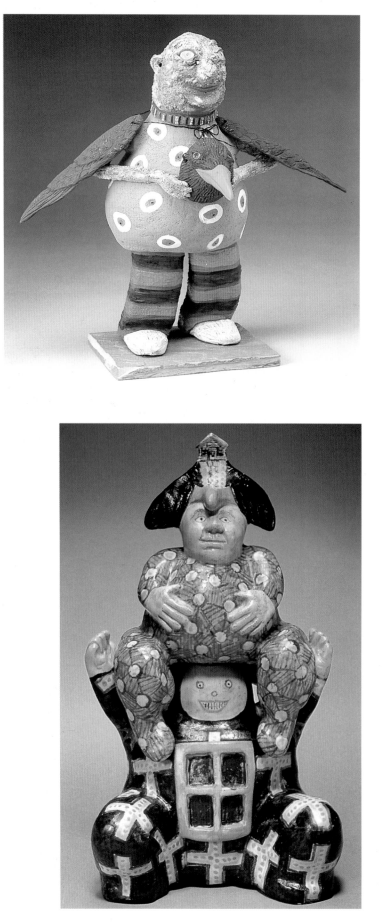

Top left: **Deborah Fleck–Stabley**, *Take Flight*, 2000. 15 x 15 x 7 in. (38.1 x 38.1 x 17.8 cm). Red earthenware; slab and coil built, textured, carved; glaze, underglaze, special effects glaze fired in electric kiln, Δ05. Photo by Mark Anderman

Top right: **Hasuyo V. Miller,** *Room Mates*, 1999. 22 x 10 x 7½ in. (55.9 x 25.4 x 19.1 cm). White stoneware; house slab built, coil additions; alligator and fish pinched, coiled; raku fired to 1900°F (1027°C) with newspaper reduction. Photo by artist

Left: **Marilyn Andrews**, *Stacked Figures,* 1997. 10 x 5 x 5 in. (25 x 12.5 x 12.5 cm). Stoneware; handbuilt; fired in electric kiln, Δ5. Photo by Bob Barrett

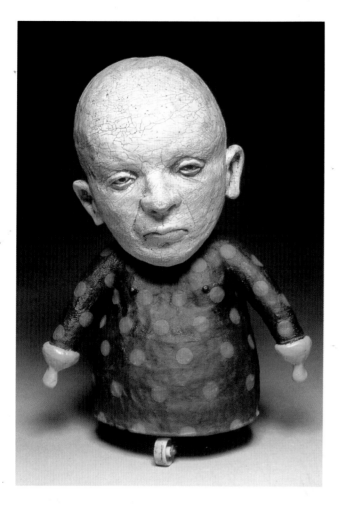

Top left: **Tom Bartel**, *Nipple Boy*, 1998. 28 x 16 x 12 in. (71 x 40.8 x 30.5 cm). Red earthenware; coil built; multi-fired with vitreous engobes, terra sigillata, oxidation, Δ02. Photo by artist

Top right: **Paul Andrew Wandless**, *Mr. Talkofpast,* 1999. 24 x 18 x 13 in. (61 x 45.7 x 33 cm). Lowfire paper clay with kyanite; pinch and slab construction; slips, glaze, textural glazes multi-fired, Δ02 to Δ08. Photo by artist

Right: **Charles Andreson**, *Hope*, 1999. 24 x 15 x 10 in. (60 x 37.5 x 25 cm). Red earthenware; handbuilt; soda fired in an oxidation atmosphere, Δ04. Photo by artist

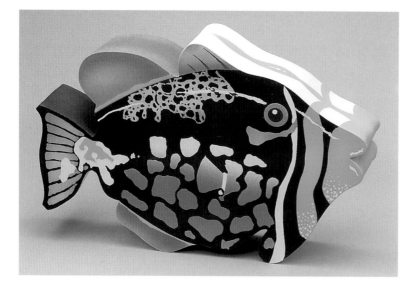

Top left: **Pamela M. Segers**, *Untitled*, 1999.
12 x 17 x 4 in. (30.5 x 43.3 x 10 cm). Low-fire
white clay; slab built; airbrushed with velvet
underglazes multi-fired, Δ04. Photo by Studio III

Top right: **Hiroshi Sueyoshi**, *Lucy in the Sky*,
1999. 19½ x 6 x 4 in. (49.5 x 15.3 x 10 cm).
White stoneware; blue, white underglazes oxidation fired, Δ6. Photo by artist

Left: **Elyse Saperstein**, *Bird in Orb II*, 1999.
28 x 13 x 7 in. (71.1 x 33 x 17.8 cm).
Earthenware; slab carved with bas-relief, some
coils; glaze, wash, luster fired in electric kiln,
Δ05 to Δ06. Photo by John Cartano

118

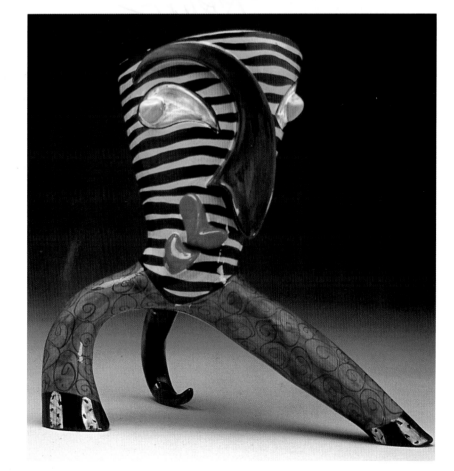

Top: **David Stabley**, *Doll House*, 1999.
16 x 15 x 10 in. (40.6 x 38.1 x 25.4
cm). Red earthenware; slab built,
pinched, carved, textured; glaze,
majolica glazes, special effects glazes,
wax patina; fired in electric kiln, Δ05.
Photo by Mark Anderman

Right: **Jude Odell**, *Untitled*, 1997. 15 x
12 x 12 in. (38 x 30.5 x 30.5 cm).
Low-fire white talc; slab built, assembled, pulled and formed parts; underglazes, glazes, sgrafitto; bisque fired in
electric kiln, Δ04; glaze fired Δ06. Photo
by Bill Kruger

Above: **Kathi Roussel**, *Lifeform–Pod*, 1998. 32 x 11 x 9 in. (81.25 x 28 x 22.75 cm). Low-fire white clay; wheel-thrown, handbuilt; fired in electric kiln, Δ06

Left: **Lauren Silver**, *Untitled,* (wall piece), 1998. 24 x 12 x 6 in. (61 x 30.5 x 15.2 cm). Stoneware; handbuilt; turquoise glaze fired in gas kiln, Δ10. Photo by artist

Top left, page 121: **Jerrold Martisak**, *Tectonics*, 1999. 14 x 7 x 4 in. (35 x 17.5 x 10 cm). Porcelain; poured slip and slab built and pressed additions; salt fired, Δ10, iron wash. Photo by Glenn Hashitani

Top right, page 121: **Carol Townsend**, *Turbo*, 1999. Low-fire clay; begun in a puki, slabs added, paddled, scraped; textured with coils and slips; reduction fired, Δ6; polychromed. Photo by K.C. Kratt

Bottom left, page 121: **Vern Langhofer**, *Untitled*, 1999. 11 x 18 x 11 in. (27.5 x 45 x 27.5 cm). Raku; slab technique; bisque fired, Δ06; fired in gas kiln, Δ06, ending with shredded paper and sawdust reduction. Photo by Mad Dog Studio

Bottom left, page 121: **Bacia Edelman**, *Red Admiral*, 1998. 15 x 9 x 4½ in. (38 x 22.8 x 11.5 cm). Mid-range stoneware; pierced, handbuilt; slips, sprayed crawl glazes; multi-fired in electric kiln, Δ04, 06. Photo by artist

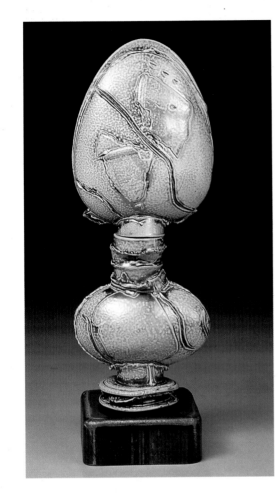

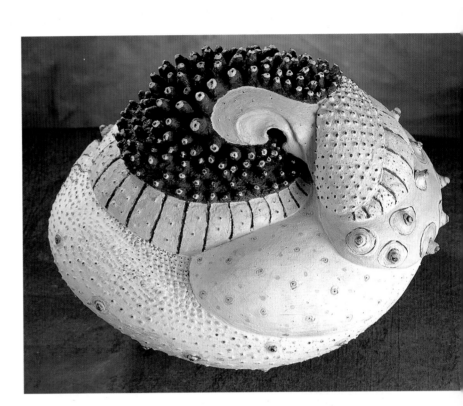

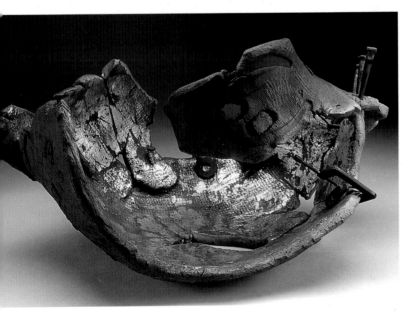

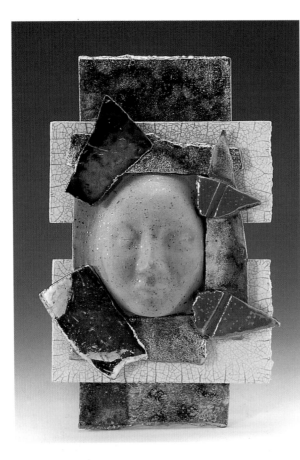

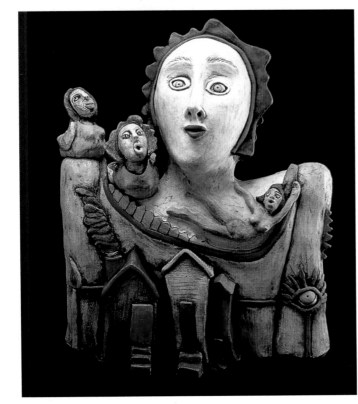

Top left: **Skip Esquierdo**, *Untitled*, 1998. 16 x 12 x 4 in. (40.8 x 30.5 x 10 cm). Stoneware; slab built; raku fired with raku glazes, low-fire glaze, patinas in electric kiln, Δ06; pine needle reduction; assembled.

Top right: **Liz Surbeck Biddle**, *Blue Phantom*, 1997. 48 x 21 x 23 in. (121.9 x 53.3 x 58.4 cm). Stoneware; coil built, pinched; terra sigillata, low-fire glazes, oxidation fired, Δ04. Photo by David Baer

Left: **Barb Doll**, *Where's Chagall?*, 1996. 26 x 20 x 15 in. (66 x 50.8 x 38.1 cm). Stoneware; coil and slab built, pinched; underglazes fired, Δ2. Photo by Bart Kastin

Top left: **Debra W. Fritts**, *Card Dealer*, 1998. 14 x 10 x 9 in. (35.6 x 25.4 x 22.9 cm). Terra cotta, coil and slab built; high fired, wire attached to box; red iron oxide stain, slips, underglazes, glazes multi-fired in electric kiln, Δ04. Photo by Bart Kastin

Top right: **Pamela Kohler-Camp**, *Horizontal Face with Leaves and Celtic Knotwork*, 1999. 12¼ x 16⅜ x ¾ in. (31.1 x 41.6 x 0.8 cm). Stoneware; slab molded, knotwork added; pressed with leaves; splashed with glazes; fired in electric kiln, Δ6. Photo by Walker Montgomery

Right: **Beverly Crist**, *Daphne Myth II*, 1996. 31½ x 11½ x 8 in. (78.8 x 28.8 x 20 cm). White earthenware; hand-built body; face punched and carved; sticks pulled; bisque and glaze fired in electric kiln, Δ04. Photo by Mike Pecorino

124

Top, page 124: **Jaymes F. Dudding**, *Arch of Gaia*, 1986. 15 x 9 x 1½ feet (4.6 x 2.7 x 0.5 m). Stoneware, earthenware; slump and hump, press molded, direct sculpture, soft slab; fired in electric kiln, Δ6. Photo by Steve Lewin

Bottom left, page 124: **Diane Dawes**, *Inner Space*, 1995. 36 x 36 x 28 in. (91.5 x 91.5 x 71 cm). Stoneware; coil built, altered; bisque and glaze oxidation fired in electric kiln, Δ04; red cement stain added. Photo by artist

Bottom right, page 124: **Patty Degenhardt**, *Mother and Child Group—Piece II*, 1999. 45 x 20 x 11 in. (112.5 x 50 x 27.5 cm). Stoneware; coil built; terra sigillata, burnished; fired in gas kiln, Δ6 vitrification. Photo by Patty Degenhardt

Above: **Victor Erazo Orellana**, *Duet*, 1997. 18½ x 15½ x 2 in. (46 x 38.5 x 5 cm) and 16 x 4¾ x 1¼ in. (40 x 12 x 3 cm). White earthenware clay mixed with paper, grog, and sand; handbuilt with textured slab; bisque fired in electric kiln, Δ06; multi-fired oxidation glaze, Δ04 to Δ017. Photo by artist

Right: **Aurore Chabot**, *Eye Catcher*, 1995. 56 x 20 x 24 in. (14325 x 50.8 x 61 cm). Earthenware, wood; press molded, reverse inlay, pinch construction; underglaze, terra sigillata slips, metallic oxide stains; oxidation in electric kiln, Δ04. Photo by Balfour Walker

Top, page 126: **David K. Morgan**, *Self-Portrait with Medflies (organic garden being sprayed with malathion to control exotic pest)*, 1993. 60 x 72 x 1 in. (152.4 x 182.9 x 2.5 cm). Terra cotta; carved reliefs with full relief carved woodblocks; oxidation fired, Δ06. Photo by Robert Wedemeyer

Bottom left, page 126: **Barbara Rittenberg**, *Moraine*, 1999. 72 x 36 x 32 in. (183 x 91.5 x 81.3 cm). Terra cotta; slab built with forms; multi-fired in gas and electric kilns, Δ04–Δ06. Photo by Joe Guinta

Bottom right, page 126: **Mary Maxwell**, *The Perfect Seven*, 1999. 24 x 4 x ½ in. (60 x 10 x 1.3 cm). White stoneware; slab built; fired unglazed in electric kiln, Δ6. Photo by artist

Above: **Dave Kellum**, *Robert E. Lee*, 1997. 11 x 14 x 11 in. (27.9 x 35.6 x 27.9 cm). Low-fire white raku clay; subtraction method on block of clay; black, white, grey underglazes; oxidation fired in electric kiln, Δ04. Photo by artist

Right: **Hiroshi Sueyoshi**, *Can You Play*, 1999. 26½ x 10½ x 4 in. (67.3 x 26.8 x 10 cm). Red stoneware; slab built; white slip, scratched, oxidation fired, Δ6. Photo by artist

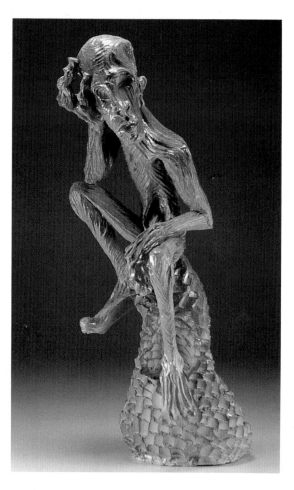

Top: **Marta Matray Gloviczki**, *Lady-Platter*, 1999.
4 x 15 x 7 in. (10.2 x 38.1 x 17.8 cm). High-fire white
stoneware; handbuilt; pressed into tree bark for texture;
partially glazed, raku fired with post-fire reduction.
Photo by Peter Lee

Bottom left: **Gudrun Halldorsdottir**, *Goddess Eir*,
1999. 22 x 8 x 6 in. (55.8 x 20.3 x 15.3 cm). Sculpture
clay; handbuilt, carved; bisque fired in electric kiln,
Δ06; sawdust fired in brick kiln. Photo by Arni Sigurdsson

Bottom right: **Mary K. Cloonan**, *W.H. Murray and
Sisyphus Do Lunch*, 1999. 23½ x 5½ x 9 in. (59.8 x
14 x 22.8 cm). Stoneware; slab built; handbuilt, carved;
flashing slip applied when bisqued; wood fired, Δ10.
Photo by artist

Top left: **Casey Thomas**, *My Inner Self*, 1999.
16 x 5 x 3 in. (40.8 x 12.8 x 7.8 cm). Low-fire
earthenware; slab and pinch techniques; pit fired
with red iron oxide wash. Photo by Carol Townsend

Top right: **Eric Nelson**, *Merchant of Muse: Ship
of Fools*, 1997. 35 x 26 x 22 in. (88.9 x 66 x 55.9
cm). Stoneware; slab built with coiled, wheel-
thrown, carved elements; anagama fired for 7 days,
Δ12. Photo by Roger Schreiber

Right: **Caryn Unterschuetz**, *Emergence*, 1998.
9 x 6 x 5 in. (22.5 x 15 x 12.5 cm). Paper clay;
handbuilt; bisque fired, Δ6; raku fired to 1000°F
(532°C), treated with horsehair and ferric chloride
solution. Photo by Bill Valicenti

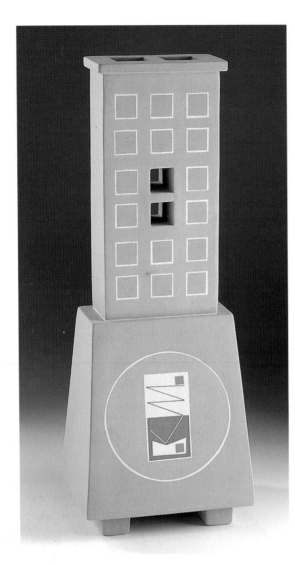

Top left: **Andrew Van Assche**; *Untitled*, 1998. 14 x 12 x 3 in. (35.6 x 30.5 x 16.5 cm). Slab-built construction; slips, washes, underglaze pencil; oxidation fired Δ4. Photo by John Pollack

Top right: **Christa Sylvester**, *Memory Box*, 1999. 15 x 20 in. (38.1 x 50.8 cm). Stoneware; slab built, stamped; crocus martis terra sigillata, copper carbon wash, low fired, Δ06, high fired, Δ6. Photo by Melva Calder

Left: **Ken Eastman**, *Vessel with White Form*, 1998. 13 x 19 x 13 in. (33 x 48 x 33 cm). White stoneware with grog; slab built; slips, oxides multi-fired in electric kiln, 3304°F (1180°C). Photo by artist

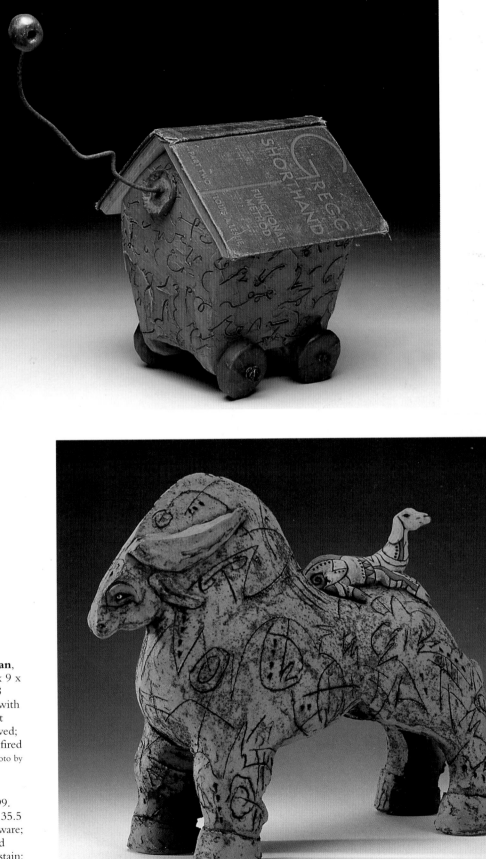

Above: **Holly Hanessian**, *Big Boy Toy*, 1998. 12 x 9 x 11 in. (30.5 x 22.8 x 28 cm). Red earthenware with found objects; handbuilt with slabs, pinched, carved; terra sigillata oxidation fired in electric kiln, Δ04. Photo by Seth Tice-Lewis

Right: **Dina Wilde-Ramsing**, *Bulldog*, 1999. 12 x 14 x 4 in. (30.5 x 35.5 x 10 cm). Red earthenware; slab built with modelled figures; engobes, oxide stain; oxidation fired, Δ03. Photo by Melva Calder

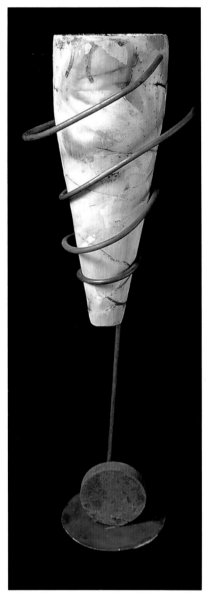

Left: **Jane Spangler**, *Elk Blood: Ihr Seit im Geiste bei Mir (I Carry You With Me)*, 1998. 54 x 24 x 24 in. (137.3 x 61 x 61 cm). Low-fire sculpture clay; coil built; underglaze, oxides, stains, black wheat, fired, Δ02. Photo by John Knaub

Above: **Mary Carolyn Obodzinski**, *Ceremonial Vessel*, 1998. 16 x 6 x 6 in. (40.6 x 15.2 x 15.2 cm). Porcelain; slab formed; salt sagger reduction fired, Δ04. Photo by Ann Nevills Photography

Above: **Pat Cronin**, *Irishmoor*, 1998. 6½ x 5 x 8 in. (16.5 x 12.7 x 20.3 cm). Raku; handbuilt with slab construction; bisque fired, Δ04; glazed with white crackle, fired, Δ06 with straw and paper reduction. Photo by John Bonath (Mad Dog Studio)

Right: **Norman D. Holen**, *Bethe*, 1975. 18¼ x 14 x 12⅛ in. (46.4 x 35.6 x 30.8 cm). Terra cotta; coil built; fired in electric kiln, Δ4. Photo by Peter Lee

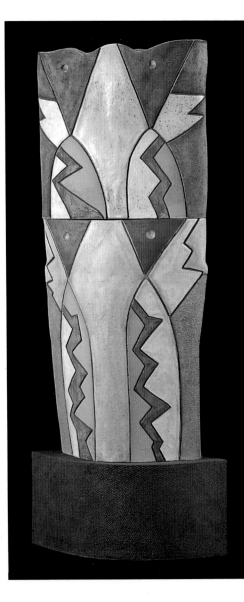

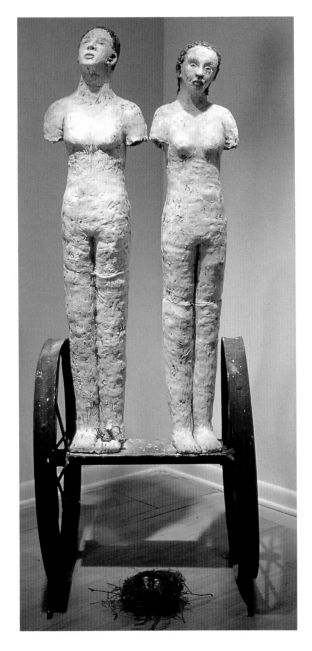

Top left: **Agustin de Andino**, *El Vuelo*, 1999. 39 x 10 inches (99 x 25 cm). Made from Δ6 stoneware; slab and coil built; sgrafitto and carving in leather-hard state; bisque fired to Δ04; ceramic pigments, oxides, and glazes; oxidation fired in electric kiln, Δ5/6.
Photos by Eric Borcherding

Top right: **Debra W. Fritts**, *Within Limitations*, 1998. 66 x 24 x 28 in. (167.6 x 61 x 71.1 cm). Terra cotta; coil built; textures pressed into wet clay; oxide stains, slips, underglazes, glazes multi-fired in electric kiln, Δ05 to Δ02. Photo by Bart Kastin

Left: **Megan Wolfe**, *Phoenix*, 1992. 40 x 38 x 38 in. (101.6 x 96.5 x 96.5 cm). Terra cotta; press molded, coiled, pinch pots, carved; bisque fired, Δ04; glaze fired, Δ08 to Δ04. Photo by artist

APPENDIX A

SAFETY ISSUES

★ Always minimize your exposure to clay dust and glaze chemicals. Some potters wear a respirator rated effective for dust whenever they work with clay that in no longer damp or with powdered glaze components.

★Keep your work space as far as possible from the kitchen and other living areas.

★ Keep your work area clean and clear of clay dust by cleaning with a damp sponge and mop. Do not kick up a lot of clay dust by sweeping or brushing. Avoid a dusty atmosphere: it is not healthy.

★ When you're working in your studio or work space, always wear certain clothes just for working with clay, such as overalls or an apron, and old shoes. Change out of these clothes before going home or entering your living space.

★ If you buy commercial pigments or glazes, always read the label carefully for contents and proper use.

★ Never eat or drink in your studio space, especially during times when you're glazing or using pigments.

★ Pregnant women should not work with clay, and children playing with clay should be supervised at all times.

★ If you do a sawdust firing, be aware that you need to thoroughly extinguish the fire afterwards. Use lots of water and be sure it is out! Sawdust can re-ignite on its own.

★ Ask questions of your supplier whenever you buy clay, glazes, or pigments. Be sure you understand what is in the elements with which you will be working.

APPENDIX B

TERRA SIGILLATA

Terra sigillata is essentially clay and bonds tightly with the clay body it's applied to. It's high in alumina, so it doesn't flow or blur during firing. Terra sig is also opaque, and as a result, you don't need too thick a coat. In fact, if applied too thickly, it can chip off. Terra sig can be applied to wet, leather-hard, dry, or bisque-fired clay. It is often a perfect finish for sculpture or sculptural pottery where utility is not an important factor. A soft sheen is achieved by polishing the surface with the heel of the hand or a soft cloth.

Terra sigillata takes on the character of the clay it's applied to: a finer clay body can result in a higher gloss than a rough body. When *sagger fired*, the terra sig will change in color according to the combustibles added to the sagger (a sagger is a fire-resistant container used to protect ceramic pieces from the flame and ash during firing).

Steps for Making Terra Sigillata
1. Weigh out the clay and place it in a container.

2. Weigh out the water and the deflocculant (sodium silicate or Calgon water softener).

Note: One common recipe calls for 28 lbs. (12.7 kg) of water in a 5 gallon (18.9 L) bucket, to which is added 14 lbs. (6.4 kg) of clay—red or white— and a few tablespoons of sodium silicate.

3. Mix the water and clay (use a blender if possible), and pass the mixture through a 30-mesh sieve; then let the mixture sit for 30 minutes. If you don't have a sieve, you can simply allow the mixture to settle for one or two days.

4. Pour the top layer into another container. The heavier sediment is clearly visible at the bottom of the container—it's generally darker in color and grainier than the top layer.

5. Continue this process every 20 minutes until there is no more sediment.

6. Test the terra sigillata by applying it to a test tile. Let it dry, and then rub lightly with your hand. If it's ready to use, the buffed terra sig will shine, and little, if any, will come off in your hand. If it dries matte and comes off in your hand, continue with the decanting process.

If you notice that the terra sigillata is thin and watery, there are two ways you can drive out the water: One is to heat the terra sig in a pan (don't bring to a boil); the other is to leave it overnight or longer, and wait for the water to rise to the top where it can be siphoned off.

Appendix C

Cone-Firing Ranges

Orton	Seger	Degrees F	Degrees C
022		1112	605
021		1137	615
020		1175	635
019		1261	683
	019	1265	685
	018	1301	705
018		1323	717
	017	1346	730
017		1377	747
	016	1391	755
	015a	1436	780
016		1458	792
015		1479	804
014		1540	838
013		1566	852
012		1623	884
011		1641	894
010		1661	905
09		1693	923
	09a	1715	935
08	08a	1751	955
	07a	1778	970
07		1784	984
	06a	1803	990
06		1830	999
	05a	1832	1000
	04a	1847	1025
05		1915	1046
	03a	1931	1055
04		1940	1060
	02a	1955	1085
03		2014	1101
	01a	2021	1105
02		2048	1120
	1a	2057	1125
01		2079	1137
	2a	2102	1150
1		2109	1154
2		2124	1162
3		2134	1168
	3a	2138	1170
4		2167	1186
	4a	2183	1195
5		2185	1196
	5a	2219	1215
6		2232	1222
7	6a	2264	1240
	7	2300	1260
8		2305	1263
9	8	2336	1280
	9	2372	1300
10		2381	1305
11		2399	1315
	10	2408	1320
12		2419	1326
	11	2444	1340
13		2455	1346

Appendix D

Studio 212 Glossy White Earthenware Glaze Δ04

Frit 3124	80
Kaolin	8
Zircopax	12
	100

Studio R Glossy Glaze Δ1 to Δ2

Frit 3134	70
Whiting	10
Kaolin	20
Silica	10
	110

Add 10–15% Zircopax for white
Add 2% black copper oxide for turquoise

Studio R White Slip for Damp Clay Δ04 to Δ6

Kona feldspar	38
Kaolin	29
Ball clay	10
Silica	10
Whiting	10
Frit 3134	10

Add 10% Zircopax

GLOSSARY

Armature. A framework used to support clay while building a sculpture.

Ball clay. A fine-grained clay that fires white or near white.

Bas-relief. (low relief). Modeling of the clay that is raised only slightly off the surface. Can be done to give the illusion of three-dimensionality.

Bentonite. A very plastic clay added to glazes to improve suspension and to clay bodies to improve plasticity.

Bisque firing. The first firing of unglazed clay at a low temperature, usually $\Delta 010$ to $\Delta 04$.

Bone dry. Clay that is as dry as possible and ready to fire.

Burnishing. Rubbing leather-hard or dry clay with a smooth tool or the back of a spoon to polish it.

Colorants. Chemical combinations (oxides and carbonates) that are used to color clays and glazes.

Clay. A variety of earth materials formed by the breaking down of granite.

Clay body. A mixture of natural clay and other structurally compatible materials that make the clay workable and ideal for firing at certain temperatures.

Damp. Clay that is malleable and plastic. It can be shaped, bent, twisted, and sculpted.

Deflocculant. A chemical that eases the attraction between clay particles, allowing the mixture to flow.

Earthenware. Clay fired below $\Delta 2$. Usually red or brown, and porous.

Engobe. A type of colored slip applied to damp or bisqued clay.

Fit. The act of clay and surface components shrinking at a similar rate.

Flint. A source of silica in glazes and a major component of clay itself.

Flux. A melting agent.

Frit. A glaze that has been melted, cooled, and ground into a fine powder.

Glaze. A mixture of earth minerals mixed with water that produces a glassy coating on the clay surface when fired.

Glaze firing. The kiln firing that produces a vitrified or mature glaze melt.

Greenware. Pottery that has not be fired.

Grog. Ground up, fired clay added to a clay body to reduce shrinkage and add strength.

High relief. A sculpture whose forms rise so far off the flat surface as to be almost detached from it.

Kiln. A furnace or oven built of refractory material for the purpose of firing clay.

Leather hard. The condition of a clay body that has lost some water but is not yet totally dry. Suitable for carving and joining.

Matte glaze. A glaze that has a nonglossy finish.

Glossary

Maturing point (or maturity). The temperature and time in a firing when a clay body reaches maximum hardness and a glaze melts to the desired point.

Oxidation firing. A firing with an ample supply of oxygen to guarantee that complete combustion of the contents takes place. This atmosphere allows the metals in clays and glazes to produce their oxide colors. Electric kilns produce oxidation firings.

Oxide. A combination of an element with oxygen. In ceramics, oxides are added to clays, slips, and glazes as coloring agents. Firing produces the colors through their interaction with oxygen.

Porcelain. A type of clay (or ware made from that clay) that is fired about 2300°F (1260°C), causing the body to become very hard, white, and translucent where thin.

Pyrometric cones. Small, pyramid-shaped forms made with ceramic materials and formulated to bend and melt at specific temperatures.

Reduction firing. A firing in which the intentional reduction of oxygen results in incomplete combustion of the fuel. This causes carbon monoxide to rob the oxides in the clay and glazes of oxygen, thereby causing them to change color.

Sawdust firing. A type of reduction firing in which the pottery is surrounded by smoldering sawdust; a trench, an ash can, or a simple brick chamber is used.

Sgraffito. Decoration produced on pottery by scratching through a surface of glazing to reveal a different color underneath.

Slip. A finely sieved mixture of clay and water that can be applied to clay surfaces in one or more layers.

Stains. Commercially prepared and refined raw chemicals used for coloring clays and glazes.

Stoneware. A type of clay (or ware made from that clay) that is fired to a temperature above 2100°F (1149°C), causing the body to become dense and vitrified. Buff to brown in color.

Test tiles. Tiles used to test the clay body surface and planned decoration material prior to firing the actual pieces.

Terra cotta. A type of clay, reddish in color. The name is sometimes use interchangeably with red earthenware.

Terra sigillata. A fine slip used to coat the surface of clay. A good choice for sculpture.

Underglazes. A material colored with stains or oxides that is usually applied under a glaze.

Vitrification. The point at which a clay body or glaze reaches a glassy, dense, hard, and non-absorbent condition.

CONTRIBUTING ARTISTS

Raúl Acero
Asheville, North Carolina
pages 6, 7, 8, 35, 36, 46, 51, 58, 70, 80, 87

Charles Andreson
Scarborough, Maine
page 117

Marilyn Andrews
Plainfield, Massachusetts
pages 22, 116

Jane A. Archambeau
Toledo, Ohio
page 98

Pam Arena
Duluth, Georgia
page 29

Renée Azenaro
Asheville, North Carolina
pages 32, 104

David J. Babb
Babylon Designs
Atlanta, Georgia
page 96

Bonnie Baer
Roswell, Georgia
page 29

Tom Bartel
La Crosse, Wisconsin
page 117

Liz Surbeck Biddle
Croton-on-Hudson, New York
pages 24, 122

Marla Bollak
Away With Clay
Black Mountain, North Carolina
pages 97, 112

Vincent Burke
El Paso, Texas
pages 18, 94

Aurore Chabot
Tucson, Arizona
pages 5, 25, 125

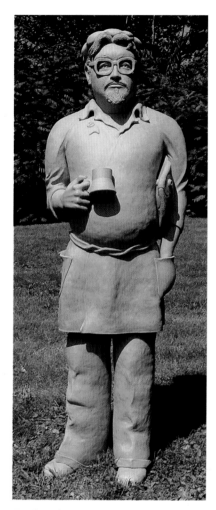

Paul J. Sherman and Fulton High School students, *Ceramic Artist*, 1992. 84 in. (213.4 cm) tall. Earthenware; coil built; parts fired separately in electric kiln, Δ04. Photo by artist

Lisa Clague
Calistoga, California
page 106

Mary K. Cloonan
Rochester, New York
page 128

Melisa Cadell Comeau
Bakersville, North Carolina
page 107

Kelly Connole
Minneapolis, Minnesota
page 34

Beverly Crist
Los Angeles, California
pages 22, 123

Pat Cronin
Lakewood, Colorado
pages 15, 133

Diane Dawes
Miami, Florida
pages 124

Agustin de Andino
Santurce, Puerto Rico
pages 103, 134

Patty Degenhardt
Fort Worth, Texas
page 124

Barb Doll
Atlanta, Georgia
pages 107, 122

Jaymes F. Dudding
Chickasha, Oklahoma
page 124

Megan Dull
Cleveland, Ohio
pages 100, 101

Ken Eastman
Eaton Hennor, Hamnish
Leominster
Herefordshire
United Kingdom
pages 99, 130

CONTRIBUTING ARTISTS

Bacia Edelman
Madison, Wisconsin
pages 13, 121

Diane Eisenbach
Monterey, California
page 115

Skip Esquierdo
San Lorenzo, California
page 122

Cary Esser
Kansas City, Missouri
page 114

Christine Federighi
Coral Gables, Florida
page 109

Deborah Fleck-Stabley
Bloomsburg, Pennsylvania
pages 28, 116

Whitney Forsyth
Tulsa, Oklahoma
page 23

Debra W. Fritts
Roswell, Georgia
pages 123, 134

Judy Geerts
Spring Lake, Michigan
pages 32, 96

Marie E.v.B. Gibbons
Arvada, Colorado
page 100

Marta Matray Gloviczki
Rochester, Minnesota
page 128

Dana Goodman
Huntington, Indiana
page 111

Juan Granados
Texas Tech University
Lubbock, Texas
page 99

Gudrun Halldorsdottir
Middletown, New Jersey
page 128

Holly Hanessian
Mt. Pleasant, Michigan
page 131

Leah Hardy
Laramie, Wyoming
pages 5, 12, 115

Julie B. Hawthorne
Hawthorne Studios
Sixes, Oregon
pages 21, 104

Steven C. Hewitt
Columbia, South Carolina
page 115

David Hiltner
Wichita, Kansas
page 98

Bryan Hiveley
Arrowmont School of Arts & Craft
Gatlinburg, Tennessee
page 9

William B. Hogan
Teaneck, New Jersey
page 115

Norman D. Holen
Minneapolis, Minnesota
pages 104, 133

Wendy James
Roswell, Georgia
page 106

Dave Kellum
Tampa, Florida
pages 110, 127

Michael J. Knox, II
La Crosse, Wisconsin
page 31

Pamela Kohler-Camp
And Sarah Laughed Pottery Studio
Lilburn, Georgia
page 123

Vern Langhofer
Denver, Colorado
pages 96, 121

Ravit Lazer
Neve Noy, Beer Sheva
Israel
page 33

Jerrold Martisak
Salem, Oregon
page 121

Linda Hansen Mau
Saratoga, California
page 113

Mary Maxwell
Kent, Ohio
page 126

Jenny Mendes
Heath Road Ceramic Studio
Chesterland, Ohio
pages 9, 20

Mitchell Messina
Nazareth College of Rochester
Pittsford, New York
pages 6, 14, 108

Hasuyo V. Miller
Ceramics by Hasuyo
Temecula, California
page 116

David K. Morgan
Mira Loma, California
page 126

Eric Nelsen
Vashon, Washington
page 129

Judith Nicolaidis
San Diego, California
page 101

Mary Carolyn Obodzinski
Crystal Lake, Illinois
pages 97, 132

Jude Odell
Handbuilt Ceramics
Indianapolis, Indiana
page 119

Contributing Artists

Victor Erazo Orellana
Madrid, Spain
page 125

Sheila Orifice-Rogers
Queen Charlotte City, British
Columbia
Canada
page 105

Pamela Pemberton
Anchorage, Alaska
page 114

Ann Marie Perry
Cheektowaga, New York
pages 6, 113

Louise Radochonski
Penland School of Crafts
Penland, North Carolina
page 17

Marilyn Richeda
South Salem, New York
page 105

Barbara Rittenberg
Larchmont, New York
page 105

Kathi Roussel
Buffalo, New York
pages 11, 120

Claire Salzberg
Westmount, Quebec
Canada
page 110

Elyse Saperstein
Portsmouth, Ohio
pages 6, 95, 118

Pamela M. Segers
Snellville, Georgia
page 118

Frank Shelton
Jackson, Tennessee
page 101

Paul J. Sherman
Fulton, New York
page 139

Lauren Silver
West Allenhurst, New Jersey
page 120

LuAnne Tackett Simpson
Imagine
Snellville, Georgia
page 100

J. Paul Sires
Center of the Earth Gallery
Charlotte, North Carolina
page 102

Gerald Smith
Buffalo, New York
page 26

Nan Smith
Nan Smith Sculpture Studios
Gainesville, Florida
page 109

Jane Spangler
Gainesville, Florida
page 132

David Stabley
Bloomsburg, Pennsylvania
pages 31, 119

Hiroshi Sueyoshi
Wilmington, North Carolina
pages 118, 127

Christa Sylvester
Clamation
Wilmington, North Carolina
pages 93, 130

Joe Szutz
Roswell, Georgia
page 20

Casey Thomas
Niagara Falls, New York
page 129

Pamela Timmons
Bath, Michigan
pages 11, 105

John E. Tobin, Jr.
PSC-473 Box 95
FPO AP 96349-0005
page 110

Carol Townsend
Snyder, New York
pages 99, 121

David Traylor
Seattle, Washington
pages 112, 113

Kathy Triplett
Weaverville, North Carolina
page 103

Gayle Tustin
Wilmington, North Carolina
page 30

Caryn Unterschuetz
SchatziBoyz Pottery
Marengo, Illinois
page 129

Andrew Van Assche
Andrassche Handbuilt Stoneware
Plainfield, Massachusetts
page 130

Paul Andrew Wandless
Blackstar Studio
Indianapolis, Indiana
page 117

Deborah J. Weinstein
Loxahatchee, Florida
pages 18, 95

Dina Wilde-Ramsing
Wilmington, North Carolina
page 131

Laura Wilensky
Laura Wilensky Porcelain
Kingston, New York
pages 10, 111

Megan Wolfe
Cleveland, South Carolina
pages 27, 94, 134

Lynn Wood
Lynn Wood Porcelain
Soledad, California
page 26

Robert L. Wood
Kenmore, New York
page 102

RESOURCES

Periodicals

American Ceramics
9 East 45th Street
New York, NY 10017

Ceramics Art and Perception
35 William Street
Paddington, NSW 2021
Australia

Ceramics Monthly
1609 Northwest Blvd.
Columbus, OH 43212

Ceramic Review
21 Carnaby St.
London WIV IPH
United Kingdom

Ceramics Technical
35 William street
Paddington, NSW 2021
Australia

Clay Times
P.O Box 365
Waterford, VA 20197-0365

The Crafts Report
300 Water Street
Wilmington, DE 19801

Studio Potter
P.O. Box 70
Goffstown, NH 03045

Organizations

American Ceramic Society
735 Ceramic Place
P.O. Box 6136
Westerville, OH 43086

American Craft Council
72 Spring Street
New York, NY 10012-4019
Ph (212)274-0630

Craft Emergency Relief Fund
P.O. Box 838
Montpelier, VT 05601
(Emergency loans)

Friends of Terra Cotta
c/o Tunick
771 West End Ave.
New York, NY 10025

National Assembly of State Art Agencies
1010 Vermont Ave. N.W.
Suite 920
Washington DC 20005

NCECA, National Council for Education in
the Ceramic Arts
c/o Regina Brown
P.O. Box 1677
Bandon, OH 97411
Ph (800)996-2322

National Endowment for the Arts
1100 Pennsylvania Ave. NW
Washington DC 20506
(Grants)

Orton Firing Institute
P.O. Box 460
Westerville, OH 43081

Tile Heritage Foundation
PO Box 1850
Healdsburg, CA 95448

Tiles and Architectural Ceramics Books
3 Browns Rise, Buckland Common, TRING
Herts, HP23 6NJ, England

BIBLIOGRAPHY

Nigrosh, Leon I. *Sculpting Clay.* Worcester, MA: Davis Publications, 1992.

Obstler, Mimi. *Out of the Earth and Into the Fire.* Westerville, OH: The American Ceramic Society, 1996.

Rhodes, Daniel Clay. *Clay and Glazes for the Potter.* New York: Greenberg, 1957.

Triplett, Kathy. *Handbuilt Ceramics.* Asheville, NC: Lark Books, 1997.

Speight, Charlotte F. and John Toki. *Hands in Clay: An Introduction to Ceramics.* 3rd ed. Mountain View, CA: Mayfield Publishing Company, 1997.

ACKNOWLEDGMENTS

Very special thanks to my wonderful editor Deborah Morgenthal, for her great humor, insight, encouragement, and editorial skill.

Thanks also to:

Art director Kathy Holmes, for her patience and for designing such an elegant-looking book.

Photographer Evan Bracken (Light Reflections, Hendersonville, NC), for his talent and good humor.

All the artists who contributed their work to this book.

And, last, but not least, Eva Renée and Luca Raúl, for giving me happiness and love.

INDEX